DEMON of PADENG

DEMON of PADENG

By Olivine Bohner

Southern Publishing Association, Nashville, Tennessee

Copyright © 1977 by
Southern Publishing Association

This book was
Edited by Gerald Wheeler
Designed by Mark O'Connor
Cover painting by Bill Myers

Type set: 9/12 Optima

Printed in U.S.A.

Library of Congress Cataloging in Publication Data

Bohner, Olivine Nadeau.
    Demon of Padeng.

    SUMMARY: Relates the experiences of a young Laotian who converted to Christianity and became a pastor.
    1. Hu Sae Yang—Juvenile literature. 2. Converts—Laos—Biography—Juvenile literature. 3. Clergy—Laos—Biography—Juvenile literature. [1. Hu Sae Yang. 2. Clergy] I. Title.
BV4935.H77B63   248'.246 [B] [92]   77-20928
ISBN 0-8127-0150-X

ACKNOWLEDGMENTS

I would not likely have pursued this story without the encouragement of Palmer and Alice Wick, who spent seventeen years working for the people of Thailand. Toward the end of those years they promoted the gospel among the tribespeople of northern Thailand, particularly the Meo. Palmer Wick first told me the story of Hu Sae Yang and the village of Nam Yawn. When in December, 1974, my husband, Jack, and I decided to visit this Laotian village, Wick arranged for Abel Pangan to serve as our guide and translator. Because of the political unrest in the area we dared stay only three days, and the Pathet Lao captured Houei Sai, the provincial capital near by, two days after we left. Short though it was, however, our visit gave me several hours of taped interviews with Hu Sae Yang, from whose point of view I told the story.

After leaving Laos, I had several interviews in Singapore with Jon Dybdahl, the one American missionary acquainted with Hu and Nam Yawn, who also knows the Meo language. His subsequent corrections and suggestions on the manuscript have been valuable. I am also much indebted to Abel Pangan, who, after we had returned home to Guam, relayed my many questions to Hu Sae Yang and wrote or taped answers to me several times. Richard Hall (known in Lao-Thai as Ahjon Hawn) took time to tape answers to my questions about his pioneer days in Nam Tha.

On the second visit Jack and I made to Thailand in December, 1975, I interviewed Hu at the Mae Taeng Tribal Center near Chiengmai. We greatly appreciated the hospitality extended to us by Roger and Pamela Kopitzke, directors of the tribal center, and the many hours they spent translating for me as I taped interviews with Hu.

Unfortunately I could not find much published material on the Meo. My most informative sources were the article "No Place to Run" by W. E. Garrett (*National Geographic,* January, 1974), and a little book printed by Chuan Printing Press, Bangkok, in both Thai and English, *The Historical Background and Tradition of the Meo,* which cited neither author nor translator. I found that both publications agreed quite generally with the customs and experiences told to me by Hu and his family.

I wish to thank my employing institution, the University of Guam, and my colleagues there for giving me a sabbatical in which to pursue and write this story. Also my colleague, John A. Spade, helped me much with his encouragement and criticism. No one influenced my shaping of the story as much as he did, and I shall always be thankful to him.

Above all the human wisdom was God's overruling hand. He took the casual intention I had of some day authoring a story of His work in Laos and strengthened it into a firm determination. First, I found myself obligated to my employing institution to write a book. Second, I had the chance to visit Nam Yawn just before the doors of Laos closed to the outside world. Third, He sent help from an unexpected quarter in my friend John Spade, who, though not a believer himself, was still willing to help me write a decidedly Christian story.—Olivine Bohner.

CONTENTS

The Valley Under Padeng —————— 9

The Talk Around the Fire —————— 29

The New Village —————————— 37

Counterattack ——————————— 59

Trial of Faith ———————————— 69

Kaifah ——————————————— 81

Danger in the Wind ————————— 101

Phua Sae Lee and the Tiger Spirit ——— 109

God Is Not Leaving ————————— 123

Epilogue —————————————— 139

Chapter 1

THE VALLEY UNDER PADENG

"Stand by the door," the father commanded, "and tell the people we are under *jai*." The shadows under his eyes and the haggard face spoke of days and nights of fear. For the first time in his life, teenage Hu Sae Yang realized that his father was growing old, that a day would come when he would no longer be the indestructible chief of Nam Chuiy.

"Watch carefully, my boy," the old man continued. "Let no uninvited ones come in. We can risk no further offense to the spirits. Your stepmother is at the point of death. It was of just such a fever that your own mother died." The memory of an old sorrow clouded his eyes. "Ten years now." He shook his head. "So fair she was, but still they took her from me." The last sentence came almost as a whisper, the closest thing to a reproach against the spirits that Hu had ever heard him say. Drawing his black jacket about him against the cold morning air, the aging chief turned to sit on a low wicker stool by the fire that burned on the earth floor.

Hu glanced across the room to the low platform bed in the corner where his stepmother lay huddled under a rough blanket. Then he stepped outside the bamboo house. As in most Meo dwellings, there was only a doorless opening. The youth leaned against the woven basketwork of the wall. His keen dark eyes followed the dusty village road that led between the thatched bamboo houses of Nam Chuiy and on north to the distant northern mountains of Laos and western China. He had never been to the end of that trail, but he had heard his father say that the Meo people had come down that road from China more than sixty years before.

Shifting his gaze from the horizon, he idly watched the chickens scratching in the dirt and the neighbor's pig rooting at the corner of the house across the road. A lone toddler, naked but for a short black jacket, lurched happily after a puppy. Turning suddenly, the dog upset the baby, who sat down unceremoniously in the road. With typical Oriental stoicism, the child made not a sound, but surveying the world from his new position, he picked up a clod of dirt and gravely began to sample it.

At any other time Hu would have laughed at the incident, but today he could not even smile. His throat felt tight and a deep aching pressed against his eyes.

Suddenly a voice to the right caught his attention. He turned to see a man dressed in Western clothes leading a small packhorse laden with two empty baskets. "*Jai, jee jai?*" the man called.

Hu recognized him as a Meo trader from a neighboring village. "The house is under jai," the boy answered quickly. "We await the *tu-ua-neng*. My mother is not well."

The man bowed. "I weep at your misfortune," he said politely. "Although I have something to discuss with your father—a matter concerning his opium harvest—it is of small importance. I will return in a few days." And leading his horse, he went on his way.

By twos and threes the invited people began arriving. They nodded at Hu as they entered. He glanced over his shoulder as they went into the dark, windowless room where his brother Yee's wife brought out stacks of low wicker stools and set them out, along with straw mats, for the people to sit on. From his station at the front door he watched as more people arrived. Most of the men wore loose black pajamas. Some had black skullcaps with bright red pompons on the top, while others had their jackets trimmed with silver coins that tinkled when they walked. The women came talking in low voices, their full black skirts swinging to reveal a border of colorful embroidery.

An hour later people filled the house. The murmur of their voices reached him at the door. Not far from him through the bamboo wall he could plainly hear the conversation of two women. "She burns with fever, you say? Ah, yes, it seems to be the same illness that she had after the last new moon. She is under the curse of a strong spirit. For this reason she is sick again and again."

Hu recognized the strident voice of Inwang Tua, the village gossip. "If Nang Blah should die," her companion answered, "that will be the second wife Yang Si has lost."

"If she does," Inwang continued in a hushed voice, "Yang Si may not last long to worry about it. Anyone knows that a woman who dies of strong spirit sickness is almost certain to become a tiger spirit, and then she returns to get her family"—the voice paused impressively—"to get them, one by one."

The listening boy shivered. Was Inwang right? He loved Nang Blah. She was the only mother he had ever known, and she had always been kind to him. Now he blinked the tears back. His own dead mother hadn't come back to haunt her family. His heart lifted a little. Perhaps the woman's story was not true. Yee, his older brother, always sneered whenever Inwang's name was mentioned. "That woman chatters like a tree monkey," he said.

Just then the tu-ua-neng arrived with his assistant, and all further discussion ended. A little man dressed in the same dusty black pajamas as any other Meo, he jingled in his hand a black iron ring strung with metal disks. Taller than his master, the assistant carried a large knife. The crowd moved aside to let the spirit men enter, and the tu-ua-neng sat on the bench provided for him. From some hidden pocket he took a black cotton band and handed it to his assistant, who blindfolded him with it. Then he began shaking his metal rings in a cloppity-clop rhythm, and everyone knew he was off on his horse to seek the spirit that had lured Nang Blah's soul away. Hu watched tensely. If the man could bring the soul back, Nang Blah would live. If not, she would die.

The rhythmic jingle continued for what seemed a long time. The tu-ua-neng, sweating profusely in the close, windowless room, grew more and more intense. He stamped his feet and called out strange words in a hoarse voice. As if under a spell, the people watched silently. Suddenly he rose to his feet. "Where? Where? Where are you, O spirit?" he screamed.

The crowd waited. For several minutes one could hear only the jangling as the frenzied man mechanically shook the iron ring. Hu's own arm ached as he watched him. It was apparent that some power other than his own had taken possession of the tu-ua-neng.

"Ah, ah, you are there," the spirit man shouted at last. "You are under that cloud. Now, spirit. Now. Tell me what Nang Blah has done."

Caught up in the excitement, the crowd demanded, "What has she done?"

The tu-ua-neng, wrapped in his spirit frenzy, ignored them. The noise of the metal rings continued, with more dancing and incoherent words. Finally he sat down heavily on his bench, breathing hard. His assistant lifted the black mask off his face. Then the spirit doctor turned toward the platform bed where until now the sick woman had lain unmoving under her blanket. "Nang Blah," he called, "you have committed a sacrilege. Do you remember? Have you pointed at the spirit tree?"

The bundle on the platform moved as the sick woman stirred. Yang Si hurried to her side and raised her head. Her face was deathly pale. She opened her eyes.

"Nang Blah, answer me! You know, the spirit tree. Did you point at it?"

"No," she answered, her voice scarcely audible, "but I remember last week I stumbled as I walked past it and—and—touched the fence that surrounds the tree. I didn't mean . . ." Her voice faded and she closed her eyes as if the effort of speaking had been too much for her.

"Ah, that was it!" the spirit man said.

"What must we do to make peace with the spirit?" Hu's father asked.

"The spirit wants to eat pig."

Immediately the chief called for a pig, and Hu's older brothers Show and Shen Dua rose from a dim corner and slipped out the back door. Hu ran around to meet them. A fat gray pig rooted behind the house, and the boys pounced on it before it could run away. Its squeals filled the air as they held its legs together, dragging it to the front door where the spirit assistant waited, knife in hand.

DEMON OF PADENG

The people crowded to the door to witness the killing. Sensing its fate, the pig screamed and struggled while the brothers held it down. Knowing a pork dinner was on the way, people grinned in anticipation. The legs were tied, and the squeals rose to a piercing crescendo. Then came the plunging knife and silence, while blood spurted over the ground and onto the bystanders. Quickly producing some spirit money, the assistant burned the paper on the body of the dead pig. Then he carved up the carcass. The head with a foreleg still attached (a great delicacy) went to the witch doctor to pay for his services, and the rest of the meat the family cut up and cooked in a big pot over the fire.

Hu looked at the sky. The sun had risen well toward its zenith, and the smell of the meat reminded him of how little he had eaten that morning. His head felt faint. From his place by the door he peered across the smoky room to the bed where his stepmother lay. The crowd ignored her. "I won't forget her," he thought fiercely as he tried to swallow the ache in his throat.

An hour passed while the meat simmered, and the people talked. Then the spirit man's assistant took down a dingy cloth bag hanging from a beam over the door. From it he took out bamboo cups and a gourd split to form a ladle. With it he doled broth into the cups, then carried them out. Hu knew he went to offer them to the spirits on a rock near the spirit tree in the center of the village.

Afterward Yee's wife and some of the other women began to dish up the meat for the people, serving it on banana leaves. Hu waited, for they must serve all the guests first. Finally his sister-in-law handed him his share, a strip of skin with a piece of gristle. The boy tried to eat but found he could not swallow past the lump in his throat. How could he eat when his stepmother might even now be dying? Crossing from the door, he stood by her bed. Her eyes were closed, but she was still breathing. He touched one of the rough brown hands. She opened her eyes. The dark blanket moved, and the woman sat up. "I would like to drink water," she said.

Her husband nodded gladly, and Hu ran to fetch the water. He brought it in a bamboo cup and watched happily while she drank, then gave the cup back to him. Touching her cheek, he commented,

"Your face is not so hot now, Mother."

With a nod she replied, "I think I am better. Bring me a little rice, and I shall eat."

Yee's wife had already heard the request and hurriedly filled a bowl, then from the pot on the coals she added some of the hot meat broth. Hu eagerly took it to the sick woman.

The crowd, which by now had begun to notice them, watched intently. "Are you really better now, Nang Blah?" Yang Si inquired hopefully.

She gave Hu her empty bowl and spoon. "The rice tasted good. Yes, I think I am well. I am glad the spirit accepted the sacrifice."

The tu-ua-neng, whose sharp eyes had missed nothing, stood up. "Great praise to *Da-nyu-va*," he cried. "As you all can see, she was healed as soon as the offering was set on his stone. You are very lucky, Yang Si. Once again the spirits have returned your wife to you."

The boy felt the release of tension in the crowded room. Suddenly all the people began laughing and talking at once, with much recounting of similar healings and of the many taboos among which the Meo had always carefully to pick their way.

Then the spirit man left, having first repeated a final lucky incantation. His assistant followed him, the pig's head wrapped in banana leaves under his arm. The people began to depart then, each bowing to the father, congratulating him on his good fortune and wishing health and favor on the family.

Hu looked at his father, who beamed at his wife. Nang Blah had thrown off the blanket, and she began pinning up her hair. Her broad face already showed healthier color. The boy felt happy that his mother was returning to normal, but he felt no thankfulness toward the spirits—only a deep burning resentment. He had often known her to have such sudden mysterious illnesses which, after a sacrifice, would vanish. "How can we be sure you will not be sick again?" he asked.

"We can never be sure," the mother replied, "but we must always try to be more careful not to offend the spirits."

"More careful! How can we be more careful? We creep about

like—like—frightened cats now. You meant no harm to the spirits when you stumbled. You . . ."

But Hu said no more, for his father clapped his hand over his mouth. "Keep your tongue quiet," he told him fiercely. "Is it not enough that your mother has just returned from death? Do you want us all to come under a curse?"

Twisting away from his father's grasp, Hu ran out into the sunlight, a deep anger smoldering in him. As the days passed, the idea of escape from the continual shadow of fear never entered his mind. But sometimes he wondered vaguely in thoughts too deep for words if he would ever have any other kind of life.

One day during the cold season he sat by the fire on the earth floor of his father's house. His stepmother had just lifted her pot off the fire and taken away the metal frame it rested on. She motioned to him to remove from the fire the long log which was burning at one end. Pushed away from the red coals, it would quickly go out, and thus they would waste no fuel. He watched the smoke from the extinguished log as it drifted up through the triangular hole where the thatched roof formed a gable.

Suddenly he became conscious of a strange noise—a steady, squeaky murmur that almost seemed like speaking. Then the rhythm slowed, and the noise formed itself into words he could recognize. He darted for the door. There in the bright sun a group of Meo squatted on the bare ground, looking at a wooden box. On its top was a disk, which one of the men turned with his finger. The movement made a voice come out, and most wonderful of all, it spoke the Meo language. Fourteen-year-old Hu grinned with delight. "Where did you get that talking machine?"

"From Nam Tha. There's an American there called *Ahjon Hawn*. He gave it to us."

"Gave it to you? You mean for nothing?"

"Yes, he said we should let it talk to us so we could hear the stories. Be quiet and listen."

So Hu did. The voice told about a man named Noah who had told the people long ago that they were bad and they needed to turn their hearts around and be good, but they wouldn't heed his warnings. So after 120 years, the great God who made the world sent a flood of water that drowned the earth and its people except for Noah and his family.

After the men with the machine had left, Hu remained quiet for a long time. He pondered a lot about evil and goodness and the need to please a good God. The people in his village—in his whole valley —all needed to turn their hearts around, he thought. He needed to be good too. But how? He couldn't seem to find the answer.

One day a little more than two months afterward, Hu was lying inside the house near the fire pit wrapped in extra clothes because he felt chilly. He was quite sure he had a fever, but he didn't want to complain about it. Not yet. Maybe if he could just rest quietly by the fire, he would get well by himself. If only he could escape the wrangling witch doctor, the squealing sacrifices, and the house crowded with people, he thought he might get well in spite of the spirits. While he did not have the boldness to say such things aloud, of course, he still wished.

Suddenly he heard strange voices and sensed some kind of excitement on the village path that passed his father's house. As the voices drew nearer he could hear both the Meo and the Lao languages. Shadows filled the doorway as his father entered, followed by several villagers and four strangers: a Meo chief, a man of the Thai Dom tribe, a Thai, and one American. At the sight of the strangers Hu forgot about his sickness and stood up. He noticed the American particularly. The man had such a kind, calm look in his eyes—blue they were, a strange color for eyes, to be sure—but Hu felt somehow that here was a man that he could trust completely. Speaking Lao while the Meo chief translated, the white man told them he was the same Ahjon Hawn who had given the men the talking machine.

He and his helpers were starting a school in Nam Tha, and he was looking for bright Meo boys eager to learn. As he spoke he made marks on a paper in his hands. "We will teach you about growing food, about healing sick people, and about the God in the sky and His Son, Yesu, who makes men good."

The young Meo was overjoyed to hear of the school. Maybe the man could tell him how to turn his heart around and be good. Perhaps Yesu, the Son of the Great One, could help him. Without waiting to consult his father, Hu shouted, "Put my name down. Put my name down. I want to belong to the school."

Smiling at his eagerness, the pastor wrote down the name of Hu Sae Yang, along with two other boys he found in Nam Chuiy, and explained that the school would start the next week. The American left, and Hu, full of excitement at the new prospect, felt almost well. He went looking for the other two boys in the village who had chosen to go to the new school, and together they made plans. They would not need to do much packing or preparation. Gathering their belongings, the boys journeyed on foot, arriving at the new school in Nam Tha in two days.

Like most Meo, none of them could read or write, and they had little knowledge of the outside world. The simple school set up by Ahjon Hawn and his assistants represented a whole new world to them. The missionaries' plain wooden house with its single wall construction and wide back porch, set up on a log post foundation, seemed like a palace to Hu. It was the cleanest place he had ever seen, and it even had water piped into it from two empty oil drums set up on a kind of tower to catch the rain.

When he had a minute to spare from school, Hu liked to watch the clinic Ahjon Hawn operated on the back porch. Here the American pulled out aching teeth, shot medicine into people's arms with a shiny needle, gave out round little pebbles to make people well, and sometimes sewed the edges of wounds together with a needle and thread much the way Hu's mother made embroidery patterns on her skirt. They never sacrificed as much as a chicken, and though the boys didn't see a tu-ua-neng anywhere, the people seemed to get well. As Hu learned to understand Lao, he heard the patients talking about the power of the American medicine.

Near the house stood a wooden chapel with a room at the back where the school boys slept and a room in the front with long benches where Ahjon Hawn held school classes during the week. On the day called Sabbath everyone met there to talk to God and to listen to Him talk back to them from His Book.

Adjustment to the new life came hard for Hu at first. The school used Lao, a tongue which all his life he had heard but never learned to speak. Every day a Lao came up from the town to teach the language to them. The boys learned agriculture, spending some time each day in the school garden. As he became more skilled in the Lao language, Hu began to enjoy the Bible classes taught by Pastor Mun, the Thai missionary. In them he learned more of the Father who made the world and of His Son, Yesu, who had once come to visit the people on earth, even becoming a man Himself. Little by little Hu began to realize that Yesu was more powerful than Da-nyu-va—yes, greater than any spirit—and that He loved ordinary people—even Hu Sae Yang, a Meo boy from a small mountain village.

The way the missionaries lived, free and happy, offered proof of what they taught. They seemed to be above the spirits—they walked where they wished, pointed where they liked, talked openly and freely. For them the death call of the *klong-lu-hao* meant nothing, going on their way as though that bird's spirit had no power to eat their heads at all. And they didn't fear sickness. The missionaries had good medicines. When those failed, they prayed to the Father in the sky, and He healed the sick. Hu decided he wanted such a life, and he worked daily to learn all he could.

The youth learned about cleanliness and healthful living. One thing that surprised him greatly was the missionaries' attitude toward opium, a product that all Meo looked upon as precious. Coming as they did from a cashless society, the Meo boys in the little school had not brought spending money with them. Instead, each had in his bundle a black ball of raw opium gum wrapped in cloth. When the missionaries refused to buy it from them, the boys sold it, pinch by pinch, to Chinese merchants in the town of Nam Tha. One pinch would bring enough ready money for a schoolboy's needs, and the ball they brought lasted for the school year. Later when Hu had learned more of God's character, he gave up even his small trade in opium.

One morning while he was in school he glanced up from his lessons. He was seeing with only one eye since the other was infected and had a patch over it. At the door stood his older brother, Yee, motioning to him. Hu quickly rose to meet him, and they stepped outside to talk. His brother wasted no words. "This is not a good place for you, Hu. Father wants you to come home right now."

Hu's face fell. Just as he was beginning to find a life of freedom and light, the thought of going back to the darkness of the spirits, the sickness and fear, seemed unbearable. "I can't go—not yet. I'm just beginning to learn . . ." His voice carried a note of desperation. How could he explain all the wonderful new things?

"You can't trust these Americans," Yee continued. "The tu-ua-neng and lots of people and—and—everybody say they take mountain people to fatten them up and—and—eat them."

Perhaps the suppressed merriment he saw in Hu's one good eye made him falter.

Hu burst out laughing. "You're the one who knows nothing," he laughed. "I wish you could just watch Ahjon Hawn day after day healing people over at his clinic. They give him no pig's head for it either. He just wants to help them."

Yee didn't take ridicule from his younger brother gracefully. "What about your eye?" he grumbled. "The spirits are angry, and they will soon make you blind. You are a slave of the Americans."

Carefully Hu explained how the missionaries washed his eye with medicine morning and evening. "It is getting better," he insisted. "It was worse last week. And I'm not afraid of the spirits. I'm learning about Vatiu Yesu. He's stronger than all of them."

"Father will be angry," the brother insisted.

But Hu could be stubborn too. "Tell him I am happy. I must stay. I have much to learn and have only started."

Because of the threat to his new way of life, Hu often turned his mind to the God he was learning to know: "Father in the sky, this is Hu. You know I want to be Your boy. I want to learn Your Book. Don't let my family take me away."

It seemed that God heard. For the time being, at least, no one else came to take him back to Nam Chuiy. Some of the other boys in the school were not so sure as Hu. When their parents, fearing the American people-eaters, came to take them home with them they went, and so the little school lost some of its students to superstition.

One day Pastor Mun told the boys about a rite called baptism and how, when a man decided to turn his heart around and begin to live God's life, he should show his decision publicly. He must go down into the river with the pastor who would bury him under the water and raise him up again. It would show that because of Yesu he was dead to evil but alive to God. Hu knew at once that it was what he wanted to do.

One Sabbath early in May of that same year, Ahjon Hawn baptized him and the rest of his companions in the Nam Tha River.

About a month later when the rainy season had just started, the missionary family left for America, and Abel Pangan, a young Filipino, came to take their place. Ahjon Pangan had had to leave his wife behind in school and arrive quickly so the Americans could get out of Nam Tha before the monsoon rains completely flooded the small airfield. Once that happened, no one could travel out of Nam Tha except by foot trail.

The students in the little school found the new pastor friendly, but he couldn't talk to them, because he didn't know a word of Lao. The loneliness and isolation were enough to break most men, but his students soon learned that the new ahjon was no ordinary individual. He set out to learn Lao by inviting the leading town officials to an English class. As he taught them English, from them he learned Lao. Hu noticed how he practiced speaking to every Lao he met. In three months the Filipino began preaching simple Lao sermons in the little wooden chapel. Also he treated the sick as Ahjon Hawn had done—pulling teeth, giving out medicines, and sewing up wounds.

One Sabbath afternoon Hu, riding his brother's horse, set out to visit a recently baptized Meo friend. He took with him his Bible story picture roll. Reaching Seu Sae Kan's house in good time, he tied his horse to a stump nearby and spent a good hour reviewing God's promises with the friend and his family. Late afternoon Hu left the house and walked over to the stump. He noticed the animal was whinnying restlessly and decided to offer him a drink from the nearby stream. Winding the rope around his wrist, he prepared to lead him, when the horse suddenly gave a wild plunge which jerked Hu into the air and hurled him face down on the jagged stump.

He struggled to his feet, conscious of a burning pain across his upper lip and the taste of blood in his mouth. Then he could see the blood as it ran down onto his shirt. Seu Sae Kan and his family came running and soon brought water to wash the blood away. Feeling faint, Hu sat on the ground while his friends kept dabbing at his face. "The blood won't stop," he heard them say. Seu prayed. Soon the bleeding ceased, and Hu began to feel less dazed.

Seeing the shocked looks on the faces around him, he tried to talk, but his lips would not respond. Gingerly he lifted his hand to touch his mouth. "Don't touch it," Seu said sharply, pulling his hand back. "Your upper lip is split open, and your chin is cut. You must get on your horse. I'll guide you home."

When the boys arrived at Nam Tha, Ahjon Pangan and Ahjon Mun were shocked at the sight of their student's mutilated face, but fortunately both had become quite skilled at suturing. In less than an hour they had repaired Hu's lip, and the boy recovered without any complications, though he always bore a dented white line on his upper lip and a scar on his chin.

News of the accident caused his father, who still feared the spirits, to send for him again. But Hu remained firm. "Tell my father that I'm getting well, and I'm happy here. I have so much to learn, and God has work for me to do. I cannot leave."

After his furlough, Ahjon Hawn brought back a small plane with him from America. It excited the boys at the school to see it and to walk up and even touch the sky machine. One day Ahjon Hawn said, "Ai Hu, how would you like to return to your village and begin teaching your people what you have learned here?"

"Oh, yes, Ahjon, that has been my dream for many days."

"I was thinking," the pastor continued, "that you could go on ahead and tell your people that we would like to start a school in your village, but we will have to build an airstrip so I can land the plane and bring the supplies in. You must clear the land and smooth it down. First, though, I will fly up and drop you some tools to help with the work."

The plan thrilled Hu, and soon he started for his village, where his father and brothers welcomed him gladly. His perseverance in sticking by his schooling had finally won out, and the family seemed convinced that he had done a good thing. At dawn they set to work on the new airstrip, felling the big trees and slashing the underbrush. About midday they heard a roar, and great excitement spread among them as the mission plane appeared and circled over them.

"Stand clear," Hu warned, and soon the bundles began dropping from the sky: baskets for carrying the dirt away and new hoes and mattocks. Everyone worked with enthusiasm for the next few days, and the airstrip began to take shape. But late one night the screams of women and the barking of dogs awakened Hu. Someone shouted, "The soldiers come," and the whole village sprang to life. The rest of the night was a wild clutter of scrambling villagers fleeing with crying infants and snatched-up bundles. Most of their belongings they left behind. Hu's family managed to grab a few treasures and some baskets of rice, but he would always remember his father's sad voice, "Oh, what a pity. I left behind my new hoe, the one Ahjon dropped to me from the sky."

Most of the people escaped, and eventually they set up a village right on the edge of Nam Tha. But the respite was short. The time came, finally, when invasion threatened the city itself, and Ahjon Hawn with his plane evacuated the school and the teacher families across to the town of Chiang Khong on the Thai side of the Mekong. Hu went with the school, but his family, with other villagers, fled yet again and established the village of Nam Vua south of Nam Tha.

During the next few years Hu crossed the river from Chiang Khong and hiked north the three-day journey up to Nam Vua several times. On each visit he told his family more and more of the Father in the sky.

Once, just before his transfer to another country, Ahjon Hawn risked the danger of guerrilla warfare and visited Nam Vua for a few days. During his visit Hu's parents asked the pastor to perform *zia da*, a service in which they had all their spirit fetishes and relics burned while the pastor committed the house and family to the care of the Creator-God. After that time Hu noted a health and joy in his

DEMON OF PADENG

family that had never possessed them before.

Finally his parents told him that they too wanted baptism. Laos no longer had any Seventh-day Adventist pastors, and with the insurgents occupying the hinterlands, it would be too dangerous for any foreign pastors to penetrate as far as Nam Vua. "I will write Ahjon Wick, Father," Hu said. "He is the mission *pookheng* of Thailand and Laos, and I will ask him what we should do."

Correspondence with Ahjon Wick brought the suggestion that the believers of Nam Vua come south to the border and found a Christian village accessible to the missionaries. After much prayer Hu thought of a possible place, the Nam Yawn Valley a few miles back from the Mekong. Ahjon Wick agreed to meet Hu in Chiang Khong and go with him to see it. Hu had walked through the Nam Yawn Valley many times, for the main trail north passed through it. Rising over it stood a wooded mountain with a rocky peak of stone—Padeng, the Lao people called it. As he continued to pray for guidance, the thought of Nam Yawn came ever more strongly to his mind as an ideal site for the new village. He knew that local legend surrounded the mountain with fear and mystery. This was why the valley below it remained uninhabited. It was fertile, well watered, and abounding in game, but the tribes people dared not live there. Some would not even camp overnight in it, journeying through it only by daylight.

Hu mentioned nothing about the superstitions to the Ahjon as the two men—the tall slender American and the young Meo with the keen eyes and determined chin—stood on the bank of the clear-flowing Nam Yawn River. "What do you think, Ahjon? A beautiful valley, isn't it?"

Ahjon Wick had a smile that wrinkled up his whole face. "That's just it," he grinned. "It's almost too good to be true. Are you sure nobody claims this land? Maybe after you settle here, someone else . . ."

"No one claims it, Ahjon," Hu interrupted. "I am sure of it. I don't know of anyone who wants to live here."

"Well, if you're that positive, go ahead. What is your plan?"

"I'll go back to Nam Vua," Hu went on, his face lighting up.

"And I'm quite sure I can persuade one of my brothers and Toon Kwa, the former witch doctor—maybe one or two others—to come back with me before the rainy season starts in May. We'll clear and burn off the land and plant rice and corn. Then we can build temporary shelters for ourselves and stay long enough to see if the crops are good. If they are, we'll bring our families and build our houses."

A few days later Hu Sae Yang took the trail leading north to Nam Vua, his father's village. He spent two nights with friendly villagers along the way, and on the third day he hoped to reach his father's house by nightfall.

It was still the cool of early morning as Hu walked along, but already many people followed the primitive road. Descending a steep hill, a caravan came into view. It consisted of Meo traders, most of them dressed in army-surplus clothes, green fatigues or camouflage-patterned windbreakers. They carried rifles as they led their heavily laden ponies. Hu felt certain they were opium traders. He merely nodded without speaking, knowing that people in that trade didn't care to socialize as they carried their contraband goods toward the Thai border.

The youth remembered his own experience with the opium industry from days when his father, with the rest of the people in his village, had cultivated large fields of poppies. Most other activity in the village came to a standstill when the weather was right and the poppy pods were ready. Everyone had to help, for they had to scratch the pods on a clear sunny day so the opium sap would ooze out properly and dry into the black gum which they later collected into black balls of raw opium. Hu knew well enough that a pound of raw opium would bring as much money as a quarter ton of rice. Any Meo farmer who could raise a pound of opium in a year felt quite satisfied. And it was much easier to transport it on the long trails than perishable foods. But despite the fact that it was the money crop, Hu knew that the new village would not grow any. He wasn't sure yet what their source of cash would be, but he had made the decision. Long ago he had learned that trade in opium meant misery for other men. "No," Hu thought, "we will do only what God

DEMON OF PADENG

can bless. We will not turn our backs on Him—not if we're going to live under the face of Padeng."

The sun had risen high on the trail as Hu nodded a greeting to a group of women who passed him. He knew they were Yeo by the red ruffled cotton leis around their necks and the black skirts embroidered in bright patterns. With some difficulty they led two large pigs by ropes. The animals kept running off the trail into the underbrush.

No pigs would root in the new village, Hu thought—a great change for the Meo people. But the Father in the sky had forbidden them to His people; they were unclean. It would be good to have a clean village free of the smell and filth of pigs.

In the afternoon Hu saw a band of Meo women approaching. Upon nearer view he recognized Inwang Tua and some other neighbors from his father's village. Most of them had a *ketchua* of rice or vegetables on their backs. They were on their way to barter their produce in the villages Hu had already passed. The embroidery on their dark skirts was quite faded and dusty, for over a month had passed since the New Year, when all the Meo bathe and get a new change of clothes.

The women greeted him cordially and stopped to chat for a minute. Had he heard that Liu Sae Chang had died? Hu replied negatively and with some surprise, for Liu—a prominent man in the village—had been alive and well the last time he had seen him. Oh, yes, he had died more than a week ago, they continued. Hot with fever, Liu had grown weaker and weaker. The tu-ua-neng had come and talked to the spirits, and the family had sacrificed many pigs, but the spirits would not lead his soul back. The body had lain in the house for eight days now, and since the full moon was tomorrow, they would bury him then.

All the women had contributed bits of information to the story, but the main speaker was Inwang Tua. Her loud, positive voice rose above every other. "The tu-ua-neng said that the sickness came because Liu pointed at the spirit tree," she went on. Her eyes narrowed, and her voice dropped to a harsh whisper. "You know, the spirit tree on the edge of the village above the lower spring. No one is supposed to walk close to it." She shook her head. "Liu was bold to point at it. A powerful spirit must live in that tree."

"I am sorry for Liu," Hu said. "Perhaps the spirit did kill him, but I am not afraid of spirits or spirit trees, because I know that the One called Vatiu Yesu is stronger than any spirit."

"You are a fool," Inwang sneered. "Besides, Hu, you are a slave of the Americans, and you bring evil to your family. Because of you, your father has burned the spirits. Wait and see. Your whole family will yet suffer some great evil." Hitching up the ketchua on her back, she shook a grubby finger at him. "Da-nyu-va waits his time. You will all die of a terrible curse." She flung the words over her shoulder as she started on her way, the other women following with half-frightened faces.

Remembering his past fears of the spirits, Hu longed to share his peace with his neighbors. "O Father in the sky, thank You for Yesu," he breathed, "and thank You for bringing me out of the darkness."

For two more hours Hu walked. The slanting sunlight touched the treetops, and he quickened his steps. Ahead he could see the last slope that would bring him into Nam Vua. As he approached the top of the hill, the hollow thump of drums came to his ears. Ah, yes. That would be the funeral of Liu Sae Chang. He had forgotten for the moment. The dusty road leveled off at the top of the hill as it passed the first village houses, their bamboo walls set directly on the ground. The smoky smell of supper fires hung in the air, and here and there a late chicken scuttled to roost or a pig grunted under some thatched shelter. The side of the village where he entered was quite deserted, for most of the people had gathered at the funeral below the northern slope of the hill. The drums boomed louder as he wound his way between the houses and the barking dogs. At some point above the thumping of the drums he became conscious of the mournful sound of the *khene,* the bamboo wind instrument always played at funerals.

Turning the corner of a rice granary, he spotted at last the dark mass of people gathered around the house at the foot of the hill. As he descended the slope he could see above the crowd the place in front of the door where the corpse rested on a makeshift platform. How long had the neighbor said? Eight days. The evening breeze carried its message of decay, the drums boomed on and on, the khene wailed endlessly. Some women near the corpse kept up a continual lamentation as they brushed the flies away. He could see the four sons gathered around their father's body, each with a bullock by his side. They hoped that the animals, when sacrificed, would please the spirits so they would guide the soul into heaven.

The tu-ua-neng bustled about. Hu didn't have to be close to know what he was saying. Addressing the body, the man took the rope of each bullock in turn and put it in the hand of the corpse, declaring each time, "Your son is sacrificing this bullock for you."

Now the witch doctor's assistant prepared to kill the first animal. The crowd moved back. The man raised his great hammer and brought it down, but the bullock sidestepped the blow with a groan, and the hammer hit the earth with a jarring thud. The crowd burst into laughter. The hammer lifted again.

Not caring to witness any more, Hu turned aside. Following the edge of the hill, he went on below the slope, thus avoiding the crowd. At last he reached his father's house. Just at that moment the old man appeared in the doorway, and recognizing him, shouted a welcome that brought his stepmother, his brothers' wives, and several of the children gathering to meet him. The first greetings over, the youth looked around.

"Are my brothers at the funeral?"

"No," his father answered. "They haven't come in from the rice field yet, but they'll soon be here. You know how the spirit worshipers feel about us who do not follow their ways. They fear our presence. We might offend the spirits. But come inside. You must be hungry after your journey."

Together they entered the large shadowy room with its smell of smoke, the wavering flames from the fire pit its only light. The old man brought the low wicker table down from where it hung on the wall, and Hu and his father sat up to it on stools. The mother set a pot of steaming rice on the table, and one of the other women brought boiled chicken and vegetables. After giving thanks to

God, they began spooning rice into small bowls to which they added the vegetables and meat.

"What is the news from downcountry?" the father asked between mouthfuls.

Hu grinned. "I have found a wonderful new place for us to live. Ahjon Wick says we must make a new village down near the big river. Then the ahjons from Bangkok can come in and baptize you. I have found a good valley." He paused and looked around, a happy expression on his face, then noticed that three of his brothers had come in from the fields and had heard his latest announcement. "It is the beautiful Nam Yawn Valley under the face of Padeng."

A deep silence fell over the room. Then one of the brothers spoke in a hushed voice, "Have you forgotten the curse of Padeng?"

"Have you forgotten Vatiu Yesu?" Hu replied.

Chapter 2

THE TALK AROUND THE FIRE

Hu was glad that, for the moment at least, his father made no comment about Padeng. Instead he began talking about the Nam Yawn Valley. "I have passed through the place. The trees are big, but there is open space between them; so the ground would not be hard to clear. I remember many wild fowl there." The old man spooned more chicken onto his rice. "Didn't you once tell us about fishing in that place?"

By then the brothers had pulled up their stools to the table and begun to eat.

"Yes, I told you how Ai Sawang and I camped beside the river on our way home last time. One shot from my rifle turned up many fish. We would not go hungry."

"I wouldn't be so sure . . ." Show's voice was heavy with doubt. "You know what happened to the Meo who tried to live there before. It was some time ago, but nobody has forgotten. They sowed rice and corn, and nothing came up. When they planted again, the same thing happened. If the spirits claim a place, it is useless—and dangerous—trying to fight them." He laughed grimly. "They're bigger than we are."

Shen Dua, Hu's second brother, glanced up from his bowl. "With all the land in Laos, do we have to pick a spirit place? We have trouble enough without looking for it."

"There's not as much free land as there used to be," the father stated. "Not for the Meo. If we move near the border of Thailand, we must find land fairly close to the big river, and with so many Meo driven out of the mountains these days, all the land along the river is quickly being taken. We would have to look far to find anything as good as this."

Hu noted the darkness brooding in Show's eyes. "What's the good of a beautiful place if the crops won't grow and the animals die?" he retorted. "We've all heard how the Meo who tried to live there lost their animals. They had bullocks and horses, and they became sick by the spirits."

The men had finished eating and now drew their stools toward the fire while the mother and the wives and children took their turn around the supper table.

"I don't know about the rest of you," Hu continued, "but for myself I know without a doubt that Vatiu Yesu is stronger than any spirit."

Up until then Yee, the oldest brother, had said nothing. The approval in his eyes as he looked up heartened Hu. "I believe that too," the brother agreed. "I believe the Creator-God is big enough to trust."

"Yes," Hu went on eagerly. "I've seen it proved again and again. Don't you remember? I told you all before how when I worked in Chiengmai, Dr. Lamberton, the mission dentist, taught me and Ai Sawang how to pull teeth and sew wounds and give medicine. As a result we had so many villages wanting us to come that we could hardly get to all of them. We always told the people about the Father in the sky and about Vatiu Yesu and how they are stronger than the spirits. At first the people were afraid to believe us.

"Then something happened in Ban Mai. There lived the family of Lia Nu Tah. They listened when I told them, especially the mother, Loo. She believed, but her husband was addicted to opium, and he was afraid. I told them to burn the spirits and trust in God, but they didn't quite dare."

The fire had burned down to a red glow and the women had cleared away the supper things. The mother drew another large stick onto the coals. Then she brought her stool over close to Hu so as not to miss a word. The flames blazed up as the wood ignited, and Hu continued his story:

He hadn't seen Lia Nu's family for some time, he explained.

DEMON OF PADENG

Then one morning Lia and Loo appeared at the door of the room where he lived with his friend in the back of the church. They appeared greatly disturbed. The mother was in tears. "Please, Ahjon, we want you to come with us quickly," she begged, wiping her eyes on her sleeve. "Our daughter burns with fever. We called the tu-ua-neng and made sacrifices, but she doesn't get well. He says the spirits are very angry, and they will not bring her soul back; so she must die." Loo spread her hands helplessly. "And now she sleeps and sleeps. She breathes, but we cannot wake her."

"Will you come?" pleaded the father. "Perhaps the God of the sky can do something. Go with us and ask Him."

"I can't leave now," Hu had said. "I've already promised to visit another family this afternoon, but that doesn't matter. We can ask the Father in the sky right here, and He will hear us. Come with me to the church." They knelt together while Hu quietly asked God to heal the sick girl if it was His will. Then Hu bade them good-bye.

Late that afternoon the couple turned homeward. Walking out to the main road, they caught a bus and rode for two hours toward their mountain village. Afterward they told Hu how all the way home they hardly dared to hope. Could it be that a few quiet words addressed to God the Creator could bring healing when hours of pleading and jangling by the witch doctor had failed? It seemed impossible.

When they reached their home road and got off the bus, they still had an hour's walk, so it had grown dark by the time they reached the village. Approaching their house, they saw to their surprise a fire burning brightly through the open door and smelled the meat cooking in the pot. As they entered, someone was setting bowls on the low supper table. She looked up. It was the girl who had been in a coma when they had left!

They stared in happy unbelief. "Daughter, your sickness has left you?"

"Yes, I'm perfectly well," she said, smiling. "I was lying there, and I must have been asleep. Suddenly I woke up and asked my brother, 'What day is this?' Then I sat up, and I knew I was all right. So I got up."

"When?"

"Why, let me think." She ran to the door, and they followed her. "The sun was there above those trees." And she pointed to the western sky.

"The very same hour," the parents whispered. And right there on the bare dirt floor of their house, they all knelt down to thank the Father in the sky because He was good, and they knew it at last.

"The next time I saw those people," Hu concluded, "they were ready to cast out the spirits in a zia da service. And God's power hasn't stopped in Ban Mai. The mother, Loo, now prays for other sick people in the village, people the tu-ua-neng has given up, and God often heals them. They too come to believe in His goodness."

Silence followed his story. Then Show spoke up. "That's all very well for Ban Mai, but I still think we can find some land to live on without planting ourselves in the middle of a spirit place. Why, it's almost as if we were throwing a kind of challenge at Da-nyu-va."

"I agree," replied Hu. "That is indeed what we are doing."

Then the father, who had been gazing into the fire, raised his head. "I have thought of someone else who will go with us," he said, smiling. "Our kinsman Toon Kwa. When we send word to him, he will be glad to join us."

"Oh, yes, Father," Hu agreed. "I have already told Ahjon that I felt sure Toon Kwa would come. I know his faith is strong. Any man who leaves his life as a witch doctor has to be a man of faith. He said to me once, 'Hu, I find that I must talk with the good Father all the time. When my mind wanders from Him even for a little while, the spirits that used to command me come back to torment me.' Yes, we must invite him at once."

The next day most of the Yang family went to work in the cornfield on a slope a little distance from the village. In midafternoon Hu and his stepmother decided to go into the forest on another hillside to cut firewood. As they started out they noticed Liu Sae Chang's burial procession starting up the mountain a little below them. Most of the men in the village carried the body in relays up the steep hillside. Hu knew they would have a long walk, for the people believed that they must bury the body near a running stream in a spot where the sun shone, no matter how far such a place might be. After the bearers and the mourners had passed at some distance, Hu and his mother went on. They searched for a tree big enough to make a good fire but small enough to drag home without the help of a horse. Finally they found one near the edge of someone's poppy field and carefully cut it so it fell away from the flowers. Then they trimmed the branches off and dragged it between them. They arrived home not too long before the burial party.

Despite the solemnities of the day, the whole village hummed with the news of the Yangs' proposed move to Nam Yawn. As the last rays of the sun lighted the thatched houses, groups of people gathered in the village path to talk about the news. Standing unseen behind the thin bamboo wall of his house, Hu could clearly hear and see them through the cracks.

"It isn't enough that they burned the spirits at their zia da last year, but now they want to defy the spirits on their own ground." The speaker, a young man still carrying the many-tubed khene he had played at the funeral, shook his head.

"Ah, it's suicide. And I told him so," replied an old man with a large red pompon on his black cap. "I told him. 'Yang Si,' I said, 'I used to think you were a wise one. You were even village chief in Nam Chuiy, and now you're behaving like an empty one.' "

"It's that son of his," commented another man who had just joined the group. "Ever since Hu went away to that American school he has had no respect for the spirits. Well, only evil will come of it. You'll see." And the speaker shrugged his shoulders, jingling all the coin medallions that trimmed the edge of his jacket.

A number of women passed by in time to hear his last remark. "That's also how I warned him," confided Inwang Tua, who had met Hu on the road the day before. Her eyes narrowed. "I told him yesterday," she announced to everyone. " 'Hu,' I said, 'you're going to bring great evil on your family with your foolishness.' Now I see it will come sooner than I thought."

The gossiping crowd passed on, and turning, Hu found to his surprise his stepmother standing behind him. "Do you hear what the people say?" he asked.

"Oh, yes, my son, they all buzz like bees, but I don't mind. They are not as sure as they seem. Many of them are tired of the spirits and are watching us. Some hope we are right and wonder, 'Is it possible that there is a God stronger than the spirits?' "

Hu smiled as she turned to light the supper fire. His stepmother was wise, he decided. Sometimes her words were as good as the solid silver bars that his father kept hidden in his box.

That evening as the Yangs sat around their fire they noticed more traffic than usual passing their door. In twos and threes the people paused a moment and looked in as if they considered entering, but then thought better of it and went on.

The mother, glancing up from her embroidery as she sat by the fire, chuckled to herself. "I think our neighbors are curious," she remarked.

"Curious?" her husband said. "We have no secrets around here. Come in, neighbor," he cried as another lingering shadow paused by the door. "Come in and sit down. I suppose you are wondering about our plan to start a new village in Nam Yawn."

A couple of people stepped in. Hu's mother and brothers brought out more stools, and everyone sat down. "You mean you really are going to do it?" It was the old man with the festive hat.

"I see no good reason not to," answered Yang Si quietly.

More shadows pressed around the door. "Come in," Hu called. "Enter the house." And so the people drifted in, many sitting on the bare floor while others remained at the door.

"But two tribes have already been driven away from Nam Yawn," protested the khene player of the afternoon, who by now had put away his bulky instrument. "I know," he persisted, his round face serious. "I had some friends among them. People became sick. Some died. The tu-ua-neng told them they had offended the spirit of Padeng." His neighbors murmured in agreement, their faces tense and troubled in the flickering firelight.

Then they heard a new voice at the door, and everyone turned as a well-dressed man entered. They all recognized Gua Sae Kan, a prosperous opium grower in the village. He wore the usual black baggy suit. But although the red and blue appliqué on his jacket

DEMON OF PADENG

was bright and new and the silver-coin buttons gleamed, the grim expression on his gaunt face eclipsed his fine clothes. Someone passed along another wicker stool to him. The visitor took it and sat down near the fire.

Then, turning to Hu's father, he came right to the point. "I hear you are planning to establish a new village in the valley of Nam Yawn." He fixed his dark gaze on the old man's face, pausing while the former chief nodded. "I have come to give you a warning. Your own cousin Tua of Nam Yu could tell you something of the power of Padeng. He was in Nam Yee when it happened. He said that he suddenly became deaf one day and could think of no reason for it. Naturally he kept hoping the deafness would leave, but it didn't. Finally after three weeks he called the tu-ua-neng. After talking many hours with the spirits, the spirit doctor learned that Tua had committed a grave sacrilege. He had pointed at something that offended the spirits."

The group around the fire bobbed their heads in the smoky air. "Hmmm," they murmured, "Padeng."

"You are right," the speaker cried. "The unlucky man remembered that the exact day he became deaf he had been conversing with his brother and mentioned, 'There is a spirit staying there in Padeng, a very powerful spirit,' and as he spoke he pointed in the direction of . . . of that place." Thrusting his hands into his pockets, Gua himself took care not to point. Then he continued. "The spirit man asked Tua to sacrifice a chicken, and when he did, it restored his hearing. Only think. The spirit in Padeng is extremely strong. Tua was not even in sight of that place, but a three-day journey from it."

The fire at his feet cast a wavering light on Gua's face, emphasizing his prominent cheekbones and dark eyebrows, while his piercing eyes, fixed on Yang Si's face, gleamed as from a fearful mask. "That spirit may be Da-nyu-va himself," he whispered.

The people greeted the pronouncement with a low frightened murmur. Then they looked questioningly at Hu and his father. Hu smiled at the serenity on his father's face contrasted with Gua's terrified expression. "I have heard of that experience," Yang Si commented quietly. "Yes, I expect it is true. We are not saying that there is nothing at Padeng. Perhaps, as you suggest, it may be Da-nyu-va himself. Who it is matters nothing at all. What we claim is that the Father in the sky and His Son, Vatiu Yesu, are stronger."

"My father speaks the truth," Hu went on. "You were all surprised and afraid a few months ago when my father burned the spirits. Many of you observed what we did. We took the spirit paper and the spirit money, everything, even the image of Da-nyu-va himself. Yes, and we tore down the spirit shelf. Inwang Tua, you saw us burn it, right out there where you are standing."

Hu pointed toward the door, and a startled Inwang dodged involuntarily as if he had thrown a visible object at her. He went on with laughter in his voice. "And nothing happened. Why?" His voice grew solemn. "Because we gave ourselves into the hands of the Father in the sky, and He has kept us. If the spirits have the power to surpass His protection, why haven't they done it? We have suffered no evil from them. In fact, quite the opposite has happened—we have had more prosperity and less sickness."

To his challenge there came no answer—only a low buzz of voices.

"We will go to Nam Yawn, and you will see then that the great Creator will protect us." Hu happily recognized the voice of his brother Yee, who had not spoken all evening.

At Yee's announcement the people began to leave. "They have set their minds," Gua said grimly. "Give them time."

"We shall see," called Inwang Tua. "We shall see." And she turned away into the night.

DEMON OF PADENG

Chapter 3

THE NEW VILLAGE

In the end the families who had burned the spirits were those who decided to begin a new life in Nam Yawn. Hu's father, too old for the heavy work of felling trees, willingly let his sons Yee and Hu go ahead to begin the work. With them went Yee's son Neng and his daughter Poah and two nephews, Bah and Keu. Toon Kwa, the former witch doctor and a man of sound sense and firm faith, also joined them. Hu was glad that he was with them. Toon Kwa brought with him his two teenage children—his son Tsa and a daughter Tsai. The company traveled light, taking with them only their knives, axes, and bags of rice which they loaded on a small packhorse. Their plan was to clear the land, leaving the fallen trees and undergrowth to dry several weeks so they could be burned and the land would be ready for the fifth-month rains. Then they would plant their rice. At daybreak one morning early in the second month, they prepared to leave.

Shen Dua seemed a little shamefaced at remaining behind; so he let Show speak for both of them. "If in the end you decide to come back here to live," he explained, "someone needs to stay and care for the property. We'll come later to see how good your rice crop is." Show stood in the doorway, the light from the cook fire picking out his silhouette in the early morning darkness. The travelers stood by the door, ready to go. Just then the mother came bustling out with two more cloth bundles. They would need food on the journey, and she had wrapped the steamed rice left from breakfast in fresh banana leaves, which she had covered with coarse cloth.

Yang Si watched quietly in the dim light. "I know your journey will be good," he said at last. "If I but had my strength again . . ." He sighed deeply. "But we will soon be with you."

"Your prayers can give us life for our journey," Toon Kwa told him, patting the old man's shoulder as he spoke. "Faith is the most important help we can have."

"We have three days of travel," Hu reminded them, "so we must leave now. Let us ask the good Father to go with us." And so saying, he bowed his head and asked that God would go before them, subduing the evil spirits.

Then they started off. Most of the villagers, as their custom was, had risen well before daybreak and knew of the departure, but preferred to ignore it. One did not wish good fortune to men who would defy Da-nyu-va. Even so, the group felt many eyes upon them as they passed between the thatched houses—eyes that would continue to watch them for many months to come.

The journey was uneventful except for the occasional acquaintance they met, who, upon hearing of their plans, would with varying degrees of politeness, call them fools. One old man stated quite bluntly that he would not attend their funeral. "Though it is doubtful that you will have a funeral at all," he added, "if one of the tiger spirits in the valley devours you." To a Meo, not to have a funeral was a serious calamity, for without a spirit doctor to haggle with the spirits and persuade them to serve as guides, the soul of the dead might wander lost forever.

Late on the afternoon of the third day the travelers came to a grassy plateau from which forested hills rose on the right. Through the trees on their left they caught the glint of the river, and as they neared the edge of the plateau, they heard the roar of water. The path twisted down steeply between rocks to the valley below. They stopped a moment as Hu pointed ahead. "This is the upper entrance of our valley," he said. On their left they saw glimpses of the river shining here and there through openings in the trees until it reached the Mekong, discernible only as a line of trees along the far horizon. "Here we are at the narrowest point of the valley," Hu went on, "but up there where those tall trees stand and the forest is not so thick, we will build our houses."

The others were not listening. They gazed to the right where a forested hill rose, its top a frowning gray peak of stone. "Is . . . is that ——?" began Hu's nephew Keu.

"Yes," Hu answered. Then he pointed boldly. "That is Padeng."

The others smiled at his courage, and they began the steep descent, letting the surefooted little horse go first. All the while the roar of falling water throbbed around them, though because of a shoulder of rock they could not see the extent of the waterfall. They came fully in sight of it, finally, as they followed the road at the base of the cliff and rounded the last boulder.

The plunging white water threw up a mist which the afternoon sun pierced with a rainbow that seemed to touch lightly the glittering river. Toon Kwa smiled whimsically. "The old people always say that the bright bow is the spirit of the sky stooping down to drink."

"Ahjon Hawn told us that the Mighty Creator first gave man that bow to help him remember God's promise," Hu replied. "He promised not to punish but to forgive if we will accept forgiveness. Let us forget the evils of Padeng and remember instead the rainbow that blesses our valley."

For some minutes they stood looking at the rushing water. Then Hu said, "The sun moves on. Come, let us go!" Emerging from the thick growth below the falls, they came into a clear space among the trees. "Here will be the center of the village," Hu announced as he secured the horse to a tree, "but now let us see our rice field."

He led them to the sunny side of the valley and a slope which he had earlier shown Ahjon Wick. "I think this should be the first place to clear for rice. Do you agree, Toon Kwa?"

The older man stooped to touch the dark earth. Then he put a little soil on his tongue. "Yes," he agreed. "It tastes sweet and will grow good rice and corn. Since we have no time to lose, we should start clearing soon. The rains may come early."

"There is only a little daylight left," Yee reminded, glancing at the lowering sun. "We had better make camp."

Hu guided them back toward the river to the spot on the bank where he and his friend had camped before. It was a grassy place where the horse could graze. After removing their bundles off the animal, they took their knives and began to set up camp. With a few swift slashes, Yee cut down and trimmed a young bamboo tree. Hu and Toon Kwa went into the jungle looking for rattan and soon returned, carrying some of the strong, pliant vines. Meanwhile Yee had lopped the branches off three more bamboo trunks. Against two large trees about two meters apart Yee held at eye level one of his bamboo trunks while Hu and Toon Kwa lashed it fast at each end to the big trees. Two other bamboo trunks they then placed slanting up to meet the lashed ends of the first. After binding them into place, the men tied long strips of split bamboo across the framework in rows, and to them they secured large leaves with tough grass. The leaves overlapped like shingles to make quite an acceptable rain shelter. The leftover bamboo leaves, piled under the lean-to, served as a bed, and the first shelter was ready. They proceeded quickly to make a second one.

At the same time the young people had been out snaring wild fowl. The older girl, Tsai, built a fire, and it was already burning nicely when Keu and Tsa returned with two jungle chickens. She set a big pot of water on its iron framework over the flames, and by the time the water boiled, the boys had killed, plucked, and cut the birds into pieces. Once the meat was cooking in the pot, they added rice and a little salt, and soon they had a stew ready.

The western sky glowed red over the trees as they gathered around the fire for supper. Looking up they could just see the top of Padeng, now red in the sun's afterglow. "It is truly a red cliff now," Keu observed. "Maybe the sunset gave it its name."

After eating they all sat around the fire for a while, listening to the river noises that seemed louder, somehow, in the darkness. The chirp of insects and the cluck and call of wild fowl, which even at night were never quite still, filled the jungle. All about them the firelight flickered against the dark trees. Suddenly a bird call rang through the air, sharp and unmistakable.

"It is the *long-jua*," said Tsa, startled.

"The bird of evil tidings," Keu breathed. "That call at night always means death. That's what the tu-ua-neng says."

DEMON OF PADENG

In the firelight Hu could see the boy's face—eyes wide with fear. "I have learned not to fear any of these signs," Hu told them quietly. "I remember when I first went to school in Nam Tha. I had lived there several weeks before a Meo I met in the village told me that Ahjon Hawn had built his house and school on a spirit place. 'Haven't you noticed the big banyan tree in the middle of the property?' he asked me. 'That is a spirit tree. In the past, people have tried to pasture their cattle there, and unseen things have always frightened the animals and caused them to run away. Or sometimes they became sick for no reason and died. I wouldn't sleep there even one night for many silver bars.'

"I went home trembling and told Ahjon Hawn what the man had said. He laughed, then spoke kindly to me, 'Little son, don't you know yet that Vatiu Yesu is stronger than any spirit in heaven or earth? He is powerful; yet He is good. That is why we can always have peace in our hearts.'

"After that I wasn't so afraid. Then I saw how day after day the missionaries' children played around that tree. Everyone walked under it, and nothing happened. So I knew that Ahjon Hawn had told me the truth."

"Read to us from the Sacred Words, Hu," one of the boys said. "Read about God's good spirits."

Hu reached into his bundle and drew out a thick, white-covered Thai Bible. Holding it near the firelight he began to read, translating into Meo as he went along.

" 'The ambassadors of God surround those who respect and fear God, and they keep them free from danger. . . . God is the abiding place of all our generations. Before the mountains were born or God created the earth or the fields, God is God from the beginning and into untold future days.' "

" 'Before the mountains were born . . .' " Keu's eyes glowed. "Then of course He is greater than Padeng. The spirit of the rock is only there if God allows him."

Toon Kwa got up to throw more wood on the fire. "We are also here by God's permission," he said, seating himself again. "That means that no spirit can touch us, for it is the Father in the sky who has led us to this place." He smiled as if remembering. "I was a spirit doctor once. You all know that. And in the years since I burned the spirits, the great God in the sky has kept me. The spirits have sometimes tried to capture me again. At times I hear their voices. But when I call on Vatiu Yesu, I am protected. Remember this, children. Our God is strong and good."

"Let's sing a song of God," Hu suggested. And he began,

> "Yesu loves me. I know it
> Because the Holy Words show it to me."

The song finished, they bowed and thanked God for His care that day and through the night. Then they put more wood on the fire to discourage any prowling tigers and lay down under their thatched shelters.

After breakfast the next morning the men first made more permanent shelters for the coming rainy season. They cut bamboo about the size of a man's arm and set four of the largest trunks in holes in the ground, one at each corner of a rectangle. On them they fastened the bamboo framework for a gabled roof about 3 meters high. Then they thatched the roof with overlapping leaves as they had done the lean-to. Extending from one side of the shelter and filling half the space under the roof ran a platform of split bamboo. The group wove more split bamboo in a basket weave to form walls on three sides. Then they moved all their bundles of supplies to the platform where they would be safe from rain and prowling animals.

It took the men two days to finish the structure. The morning of the following day they set out with their axes to the slope where they hoped to plant their rice. Before darkness came they had managed to fell several large trees. Late in the afternoon Yee and Toon Kwa felled one last giant tree. When it came crashing down, they realized the great space it left against the sky. Suddenly they stood in the open with Padeng looking down on them from across the valley. They both gazed at the gray rock face a moment.

"Well, he hasn't said anything yet," Toon Kwa grinned.

"We plant our rice soon," Yee added. "Then when the rains

start, that should tell us who is really the spirit pookheng around here."

With only three grown men to do the heaviest work, the clearing of the land went slowly. Three weeks passed after they arrived in the valley before they had cleared an area large enough to plant a year's supply of rice. Finally, one day they stood back surveying the results of their work. "We are now at the end of the second month," Hu said. "When shall we burn the field?"

"It will require at least a month to dry," Toon Kwa observed; "that is, if no unseasonal rains come."

"That will bring us to the fourth month," Yee concluded.

They left their field then, the slope crisscrossed with giant fallen trunks, and day after day the hot sun dried the leaves until they were withered and the piles of underbrush turned brown.

While the men had been clearing the land the young people had not been idle. The four boys—Keu, Tsa, Neng, and Bah—cut and trimmed bamboo logs in preparation for the building of the houses. Hu directed and encouraged them daily, for they would need a large pile of bamboo for the walls. Next they gathered long tough grass and spread it to dry, later to tie into bundles to thatch the roofs. While the boys and men kept busy at their tasks, seventeen-year-old Tsai, the older girl, spent much of her time cooking. She lit the morning fire, carried water from the river, and put on the pot of rice for breakfast. After the meal she went to snare chickens for supper. Sometimes one of the men would shoot into the stream, and she and the children would snatch up the fish that floated to the top.

Everyone looked forward to the end of the day when they gathered about the fire to report on their activities and to plan future projects. One night Hu made an announcement: "We are now beginning a new life. Since we are no longer in the mountains but close to the provincial capital of Houei Sai, you young people need to know Lao, the language of the country. If you know Lao, you can get along in Thailand, just across the border. From now on for an hour every night I am going to teach it to you. Toon Kwa speaks Lao, too; so he will help me."

Hu proceeded to pronounce single words for them and to have them repeat them after him. Then he went on to full sentences. During the day the children practiced Lao among themselves. After the language lesson, the evening ended with a story from the Bible, some songs about God, and a prayer thanking Him for protection.

Two weeks after the men finished clearing the slope, and while the vegetation was drying, the whole group went back to the old village to report their progress and replenish their food supply. When they returned to the valley, Hu's father and mother came with them, along with Toon Kwa's wife, Inchai, and their younger children.

They gathered around the fire that night full of happy excitement. After the children had showed off their knowledge of Lao, the men began making plans for burning the slope, while the children chattered at the prospect. For them, burning off a field represented something of a celebration.

"The leaves are almost dry enough," Yang Si observed. "Some of the underbrush needs a few more hot days."

"Yes," said Toon Kwa. "If there are no unseasonal showers, I think we should plan to burn the hill in three days."

"O-o-oh," squealed the children.

"There will be high flames," Neng cried, his eyes sparkling in the firelight.

Toon Kwa laughed. "It will be only if there is no rain. Also there must not be too much wind that day."

"That will be the second day of the fourth month," commented Yee. "After that we must wait for the first rains before we plant the rice. That may take four weeks more."

The mother had been listening with a happy face. Now she rose to bring another branch for the fire. "We can plant the corn as soon as the field stops burning," she reminded them.

"Yes, that is right," the father agreed. "Drop the corn while the soil is warm, the old people always said."

The day set for the burning dawned clear with just the right amount of wind. "We will start when the sun is at its height,"

Toon Kwa said, "because the wind will be high enough then to carry the fire up the slope."

At noon everyone gathered at the foot of the hillside while the men came with blazing torches and started the fire. The breeze snatched the flames, sweeping them over the dry crackling leaves. The children jumped up and down in excitement. Smoke rolled up off the hillside, and for a while it dimmed not only Padeng, but even left the red disk of the sun sulky in a copper sky. The fire burned the heaviest undergrowth, leaving bare patches of earth here and there, and by midafternoon it had almost died out. The earth was still hot, the tree trunks charred and smoking.

Hu's mother, with Inchai and Tsai, waited with the corn. Choosing a corner on the lower slope, they hoed the soil into small hills, poked each hole with a stick, and planted three or four kernels in each mound. The children followed them, laughing as they wriggled their toes in the warm black earth. Nang Blah hoed a mound, then handed some kernels to nine-year-old Poah who stood beside her. "Here, little daughter, you plant some." The girl smiled and eagerly obeyed.

Poah held out her hand for more kernels. "Why does the corn grow without rain?" she asked.

Nang Blah handed her more grain and began hoeing the next hillock. "While the fire was burning, some of the water from the tree trunks went back into the ground. It is enough for corn. But before we plant the rice, we must wait for the first rain to wash the soil."

By sunset they had planted the corn and everyone returned to camp with real satisfaction. "Now all we need is rain," Yee told them, "but that will not be for some weeks yet."

One morning a few days later the children came running to report that the corn had sprouted. "Just the tips of its fingers," Tsai said, her eyes dancing, "but it's up. It's up all over the place that we planted."

Her surprise and delight made Hu wonder. "Did you doubt that it would grow, little one?"

The girl blushed and grinned, looking down at her bare toes. "But all the people in Nam Vua—they all kept saying that nothing

grows here." Her voice faded, and she turned away in confusion.
"Tsai," Hu addressed her kindly, "we are Christians. Yesu is the Lord of the earth. We belong to Him. Nothing can touch us without His permission. Can you remember this?"

"Yes, yes," she said. "I will." And with that she picked up a water jug and ran off, saying that they needed more water for cooking.

Hu realized, then, that the old fears haunted the children more than he had thought. That night they spent longer than usual repeating God's promises. "Now I will teach you a song," Hu said. "When you feel afraid, sing it wherever you are.

> "Yesu is my good friend.
> He carries all my troubles.
> No one loves me as far as Yesu.
> He helps me escape the spirit's power,
> And holds me in His arms.
> No one can make me afraid."

As they waited the several weeks for the rainy season to come, they spent the time preparing material for the new houses. Fourth month went by, and they had gone well into fifth month before the showers came. Most satisfying it was to lie on the dry leaves on the platform under the thatch, listening to the rain as it came pattering on the roof, hissing along the river, and roaring in the treetops. The morning after the first rain dawned wet and gray, and they had to dig a new fire spot, for the old one had gotten wet despite the roof. But a festive air pervaded the group. The boys brought out the dry kindling from under the platform and soon had a bright fire blazing. Tsai set the pot of rice on to cook.

"With rain like this, we should soon have a fine green rice field," the father said.

"To be sure. And in the Nam Yawn Valley too." Toon Kwa smiled as he dished himself some rice from the black cooking pot.

Tsai glanced in the direction of Padeng, but gray mist completely veiled the peak.

DEMON OF PADENG

The following morning the women and children, since it was not hard work, did the rice planting. They carried baskets of rice seed to the slope, and each taking a section of the field, began to scatter the grain over the blackened earth and among the fallen logs. Finishing the planting long before noon, they returned to camp content. "Now we need more rain," the mother said. "But we don't know this valley yet; so we cannot be sure what the rainy season is like." After the first heavy rain, no more fell for over a week.

"The weather is good for building," the father observed, "but not for growing rice."

They all prayed for God's blessing on the crop, and while they prayed, they worked, soon becoming completely involved in planning the new village. "It is a good way to show our faith," Hu remarked simply. Already they had cleared the land back from the river to where the center of the village would be. Then they began to talk about the first permanent house.

"It must be a large house," the father reminded them. "We will all live together in it until we finish the others; and until we build a special house for God, we will need it for worship on the Sabbath day."

Hu remembered how in Nam Vua his father had located his house, according to Meo custom, so that they could see a distant mountain from the front door. Also, the spirits had approved the site. To learn the spirits' will, they had dug a saucer-shaped indentation on the proposed site and placed grains of rice—one for each member of the family—in it. If the spirits had not moved the grains by morning the family considered the site approved.

"We are free now," his father said as they walked over the ground. "Free to follow our own good sense and to build where we see fit." With a sweep of his arm he indicated a grassy plot of ground. "Let us build here. The ground is quite level and high enough to remain dry in rainy season, and yet we are not too far from the river."

The men agreed and accordingly measured off a rectangle 10 by 12 meters in area. Hu stood at one corner. "The doors can be here and yonder." He pointed across the house area. When they finished the house, it would be on the one spot from which they could *not* see the most prominent mountain. "We give no respect to Padeng in this house," he explained. And the others nodded in agreement.

The next step required finding trees of the right size for corner posts and framing. Soon the men had trimmed them of branches and carried the timbers to the building site, where they set them in the ground. Succeeding days saw the hardwood framework for the roof raised. Next they thatched the roof with tough grass stitched together in bundles. Last of all they wove the walls of split bamboo and bound them to the corner posts. By the end of the week the house was snug, watertight, and ready for occupancy.

It was then that the rainy season really began. The second day after the rains returned, the rice sprouted up all over the field, but it was evident that not all of it had germinated. "The week of dry weather right after the planting did it," Toon Kwa said, "but I think we will still have enough."

"God is watching this field," Hu declared. "We don't have the harvest yet, but God has promised to supply our needs, and I know He will not fail." In the late afternoon sun the little blades shone with such a lively green that to Hu it seemed that some inner light illuminated them.

As they turned toward camp they all observed how clouds veiled Padeng. "I'd hide my face, too, if I were you," Keu laughed, and the others joined him.

A few days later most of them prepared to return to Nam Vua for the final move. Toon Kwa's family and some of the boys remained behind to keep watch on the rice fields, replanting where birds or field rats had eaten the seeds. They also continued gathering material for the next houses.

The evening of the third day after their departure, the group arrived in Nam Vua under the quietly curious gaze of their neighbors. They had come back safe and whole for all to see, but the villagers made no comment beyond a few careful questions about weather and crops. When the pioneers told of their successful rice field and of their progress in building, the whole village buzzed with the news. Few questioned them at any length, but Hu thought he could detect a kind of chastened caution on many faces. Nothing has hurt you yet, perhaps, they seemed to be saying, but just remember the five months until the harvest.

The excitement of moving, however, kept the Yang family too busy to worry much about the reaction of their neighbors. In a surprisingly short time they had the caravan ready. Several small packhorses stood loaded with bundles of clothing, ketchuas of rice, basket stools stacked and tied together, cooking pots, and garden tools, as well as a chest of silver bars and the precious silver neck rings which determine every Meo woman's wealth and worth. Last of all they gathered up the family chickens, each closed in its individual wicker basket. With the chickens tied onto the horses, they set out in the gray of early morning.

As before, the villagers offered no farewells, and Show and Shen Dua remained behind in the old house. "We will come after you have a harvest," they said. "And someone must tend the fields here." What they said, of course, was true, so neither group reproached or ridiculed the other.

"They will come when their faith has grown," Hu confided to his mother as they trudged along, each leading a laden horse.

"I am sure of it," she said. "And not only they, but others in Nam Vua. Why, only last week Niu—the son of Liu Sae Chang, who just died—asked me, 'If you get a good harvest in Nam Yawn, would you let some other people move into your village also?' I said, 'May God make it so. Anyone who trusts the Father in the sky will be welcome.'"

"I'm glad to hear it," Hu replied. "I'm sure there are others like him. That man had to sacrifice a bullock and many pigs for his father's sickness and death. He is weary of *da* worship. Once we are really established in Nam Yawn, we will have a light that shines all over this country. The road going by our village is the main trail. Caravans will stop. They will ask questions. We will tell them about what Vatiu Yesu has done for them." And Hu's face shone at the prospect.

They had been permanently settled in Nam Yawn only a few weeks when they noticed that something wonderful had happened in the rice field. The crop that had seemed sparse at first began to look prosperous. Each sprout had reached up and branched out to produce more grains per plant than even the father could ever remember seeing.

"It must be," Yee said in glad surprise, "that the dry time caused the field to thin itself naturally. If all continues well, we will have the best crop we have ever had."

"It is even as the Father has promised," Yang Si commented, chuckling softly to himself. "Everything that happens is for our good, if we love Him—everything. I wondered about it when the sprouting was poor, but now I see."

"The rains were good while you were gone," Toon Kwa added.

"We have a wonderful God," Hu said reverently. "Let us thank Him." And they knelt there on the damp earth to thank the Father in the sky because, as Hu concluded, "You are good and Your care is strong and faithful."

The process of building houses and settling the families continued. Frequent rains delayed the work, but at the end of the first month, they had finished three sturdy bamboo houses, and the families began to feel at home. A corral and thatched shelter provided for the horses, and the wives planted vegetable gardens near their back doors. They wanted their cabbage, green onions, and sweet potatoes close to their fires and cooking pots. Against the walls of the houses and sheltered by the wide eaves, they set round baskets, each one standing on its own wooden prop. During the day the chickens used them for laying nests. At dusk the women fastened them up under the eaves, and there the chickens roosted all night, safe from snakes and dogs.

"We have no pigs now," Toon Kwa said one day. "Where are we to find any fat for cooking?" The village adults were making a small thatched building on posts—a rice granary for the harvest. While Toon Kwa split long strips of bamboo with his big knife, his wife Inchai wove them into basketwork for the walls.

"We must buy some oil, I suppose," she answered, a worried look on her usually placid face. "But when our *kip* are gone, we cannot buy anything more unless we use the few silver bars we have hidden."

DEMON OF PADENG

From his perch under the roof beams Hu looked down at her. He and his father were binding the gable timbers together. "Don't fear, Inchai," he encouraged. "I don't think any of us will have to use our silver. Have you seen how well the rice grows? We will have plenty for ourselves and to sell."

Nearby, Nang Blah had piled up firewood under the eaves of her house. She came over now, smoothing down the narrow, blue-bordered apron that she wore over her dark baggy pants. As Hu spoke about the rice her broad face broke into a smile. "You must remember, Inchai, that the Creator is especially blessing this village. I know we will have money, not only for oil, but for cloth and even new knives and cooking pots."

Hu came down from the roof and began to hand up some of the bamboo strips so his father could fasten them across the beams. Next, they sewed bundles of tough grass to them for thatch. "There is more than one way to have money," the father remarked. "A man can sell things or he can have money by not spending much. We sacrifice no animals. In the end we make money."

"You are right," Toon Kwa said. "The year before I burned the spirits, we killed thirty chickens and nine pigs at my brother's funeral. And the year before that I offered sacrifices for my sister's sickness—I cannot begin to count all the animals."

Toon Kwa helped his wife lash the woven walls to the corner posts. "This will be a fine rice house," Inchai observed.

"Yes," said Hu, "and we will need more than this one by the looks of the rice field."

The next day Hu set out for Chiang Khong in Thailand. The journey required more than a one-hour hike to outer Nam Yawn, then a half hour to the Mekong, and another two hours downstream by riverboat. He wanted to mail a letter he had written to the mission in Bangkok. The message stated, "Three families have now settled in Nam Yawn. Our houses are built, and the rice grows well. Six people are ready to be baptized."

As Hu entered Nam Yawn on his return, he immediately sensed some excitement. He heard high voices, children's squeals, and laughter. In the central yard where the three houses fronted, everyone in the village had gathered. Toon Kwa and Yee had evidently just returned from hunting. On a pole between them they carried a young deer, its four feet tied together. Just as Hu came up, they set it down. The animal was quite dead, but no trace of blood or bullet wound scarred it. "How did you kill it?" he asked.

The two men grinned at each other. "We didn't," they answered.

Everyone shouted questions at once, and the hunters laughed at the excitement. "We saw a big python," Toon Kwa explained. "Found it quite sleepy lying on the jungle path about two hours from here. It had just swallowed the deer, though we didn't know what was inside it at first. All we saw was a great mound in the python. So we chopped the snake in half with our axes and pulled out the deer. The snake had only just eaten it. See? The skin is still in good condition. And . . ."

"Well, let's not stand here," Yee interrupted, picking up his end of the pole. "We must go to Houei Sai now before the meat goes bad. I'm sure we will get a good price for it in town." And they strode off, hiking for three hours into the provincial capital.

The two men returned late that night elated, for they had sold the deer for one thousand kip, enough to buy a good supply of rice bran oil for the family cooking. "You see," Toon Kwa reminded his wife, "it is even as Nang Blah said. We do not have to spend our hidden silver to buy oil."

In time Hu received word from Bangkok that a pastor would come for the baptism. Since Ahjon Wick had gone to America on furlough, Ahjon Smith would substitute. The families at once began to make ready. Friday, the day of the guest's arrival, the four men of Nam Yawn walked out to the Mekong to meet the small riverboat that would bring their visitor. Hu had known the pastor before in Chiengmai and welcomed him warmly.

The next day, Sabbath, found the people of Nam Yawn gathered for worship in Hu's father's house. Ahjon Smith spoke to the people in Thai while Hu translated. Then everyone went down to the river. Gathering on the bank near a clear pool, they sang and were glad, for they had left their old village despite the ridicule of their neighbors and traveled far, braving evil spirits, to come at last to a good place. And so the American pastor baptized Yang Si, his wife, Toon Kwa and Yee, and their wives.

Some two months after the baptism came the rice harvest. It was, even as they had foreseen, the best of their lives. Everyone worked from early dawn until night. Afterward they threshed the rice. For the task the men constructed a treadmill fashioned from a slim log to which they had lashed a block to make a hammer. The log was then poised on another block so that it could be raised and lowered when someone trod on the short end. A wooden tub of rice was put under the hammer, and Nang Blah, Inchai, and Yee's wife, Lea, took turns treading the mill all day. It was tedious work, but there was no complaint—only rejoicing and thanks to God for the good harvest. When they sold the surplus rice, they were able to buy extra things they could not produce themselves.

As Hu had foreseen, many tribespeople passed by the village on the trail from the mountain country to the flatlands along the Mekong. Most of them believed in the malevolent power of Padeng and showed great interest in the fate of the Christians who had defied the dark powers. The Meo were especially interested, but of all the people, none had such intense curiosity about them as did their old neighbors of Nam Vua.

"And you are really telling me that you are all alive yet and no one sickens?" It was the old man who more than six months before had sat by their fire in Nam Vua and tried to dissuade them from moving to Nam Yawn. He was passing by with two of his sons on his way home from Houei Sai, where they had bought supplies.

Yang Si smiled as he looked up from the ax he was sharpening. "It is indeed the truth. We have had even less sickness here than in Nam Vua. But that is not all. Have you seen our rice crop?" He led the men to the first rice house and slid back the door to show the wicker bins of rice. "And that is not all," he said again, pointing to the other granaries that the villagers had built.

"What my eyes see I must believe," responded the old man. "But how can this happen? Why do the spirits sleep?"

Yang Si loved to answer that question. "Have you forgotten so soon, my friend? It is even as I told you before. The Creator-God is stronger than the spirits, and He cares for His children."

"It is truly wonderful," one of the sons admitted. "You must make great sacrifices to this Spirit."

"No, we kill no animals for Him. Long ago He required it, but now He tells us in His Book that since His Son came and gave Himself as a sacrifice, we no longer need to slay animals. The blood of Vatiu Yesu is good for all time."

"This is very strange," said the second son. "Why should a God who is so strong let Himself be killed?"

"That is exactly what proves His love," Yang Si answered. "If He had been weak, we would know His death was only a sad thing. But since He is so strong, we know His death proves that He gave Himself because He loves us."

The travelers shook their heads and returned to their laden horses. For the time being, the rice crop impressed them more than Yang Si's strange beliefs, and they went on their way to tell the news of the powerful, rice-growing God of the men of Nam Yawn.

When Show and Shen Dua heard of the good rice crop in the new village, they came to see, even as they had promised. Nor did they arrive alone, for their neighbor Niu Sae Chang came with them. With great curiosity all three inspected the settlement, the river with its plentiful fish, the three solid houses, the well-filled rice granaries. "The Creator-God has been with you," Show agreed at last. "This is a good place. I will build my house here too." And Shen Dua said the same.

"What about you, Niu?"

"If you and your father are willing . . ." The man glanced down as he stirred the dust with his toe. "You know I am not a Christian yet . . ."

"I will talk to my father," Hu replied.

That evening Hu and his father, as well as Toon Kwa and Yee, discussed the problem of new members for the village. They decided that they would not require them to be baptized or even burn the spirits, but they must show interest in trying the new life and should understand that if they definitely decided after a time they did not want Christianity, they should leave. New villagers must also agree not to raise pigs or opium, and men must limit themselves to one wife."

"We force no one to live here," Yang Si concluded. "If families choose to come, they must agree to live by God's laws."

"There is something else," Hu added. "We must not be held to their jai, or there will be trouble if we pass their door or, unthinking, enter houses when their people are sick."

The men all agreed to the last requirement, and so they established the policies for new villagers. Niu Sae Chang and the brothers, after agreeing to the conditions, set to work building their houses and soon brought their wives and children to Nam Yawn. The number of houses doubled, and people began to consider Nam Yawn as a village in that part of the country.

Not long after the three new families arrived, passing travelers brought word that fighting in the mountain provinces had renewed in intensity. Because of their discipline, courage, and knowledge of the mountain terrain, the government wanted Meo men in their army. One evening Show and Niu returned from Houei Sai full of talk about the government recruiting officer they had seen. "He says the government forces need us immediately." Show set down his bundle and leaned against the house.

"They'll pay us real cash," Niu added. "More than I make growing rice, I can tell you."

"The uniform is new," Show went on. "And the soldiers all get new black boots."

In a few days all the men in the village left to join the army—all except Hu and his father, who remained to care for the women and children. Thus Hu, when he decided it was time to build a meetinghouse a few weeks later, found himself, for all practical purposes, quite alone.

"I'll manage, Father," he said to the old man. "You have those pains in your chest. I'm afraid your heart is not good; so you must not swing an ax. I'll go. God will help me."

So Hu set out for the jungle to find suitable trees to cut for the framing. He was followed by the village children, none of whom were strong enough to be of much help where Hu needed muscle. Hu had decided that the posts must be of good hardwood, resistant to insects. He knew the kind he wanted—*donyong,* a wood so dense and heavy that it sank in water like stone. Finally, on the mountainside about a kilometer from the village he found the trees he sought and proceeded to fell them. They were hard and took much chopping, but he finished after two days of laborious work. Then he spent another day lopping off the branches and trimming them. When done, he had twelve logs each about 30 centimeters thick and 4 meters long.

He had been so intent on his work that he had not thought about anything but the job at hand. As he finished his cutting, the problem struck him. How would he ever carry them? Now he wondered and prayed as the children watched him.

"What's wrong, Uncle Hu?"

"Can't you carry them?"

"Here, I'll help you." Yee's son Neng went to one log and put his arms around it. A moment later he laughed and stood up. "It won't move."

Hu studied the logs for several moments. Then he seemed to feel a strong confidence that said to him, "You can do it. Try."

"Yes," he mused. "I think I can. First I'll get a strong forked branch and lift one end of the log with it so that I can put my shoulder under it." And this he did, balancing each log on his shoulder as he carried it to his building site.

"Oh," the children cried. "Uncle Hu is very strong." They all followed him, scampering and chattering along the path.

It took him two days to transport all the logs. He placed them in the deep holes he had dug for them at the corners and along the foundation he had marked out. Next he cut some bamboo and constructed a split bamboo floor. The women helped with the weaving of the walls and thatched roof. Simple though the building was, the villagers found greater blessing and reverence in having a separate place in which to worship.

A few months after they finished the meeting place, Ahjon Wick, who had returned from America, paid his first visit to the new village. On the Sabbath he spoke to the villagers as they gathered in the little church. He preached in Thai, and Hu translated. The pastor told of his great joy at seeing his dream for them come true. "You had faith in God's promises," he said, "and God honored your faith by bringing the curses of the spirits to nothing. For this we rejoice and thank God, but I would do wrong not to warn you.

"Now that rice is plentiful and your fields prosper, it is easy to forget how God is our keeper every moment. Things are well not only because of our cleverness and hard work but because of His mercy. The spirits cannot pass His protection as long as we remember that God is our strength.

"If we forget this, the evil spirits will attack again. They may not come in the old ways. You know too much to let them deceive you into making sacrifices or calling the spirit doctor. But the spirits tempt all of us to ignore God's commands, and when we lose faith and disobey Him, we open the way for the enemy to harm us."

The people listened attentively, but Hu above all others remembered the warning words: "Whenever we disobey God, we make a way for the enemy to enter." Would the enemy by some means yet unforeseen harm his beloved village?

Chapter 4

COUNTERATTACK

Hu, in Bangkok for pastoral training, listened to Ahjon Geo, a Thai pastor, as he solemnly related recent happenings in Nam Yawn.

"A bird cried in the night," Ahjon Geo continued, then paused to press his hand to his head in a helpless gesture. "It is not clear in my mind anymore. At that time I knew nothing about the meaning of that sound to the Meo people."

"Yes, yes," Hu answered, "that was the long-jua, the bird of evil tidings. And what then?"

"Well, you see, everyone sitting in the house suddenly grew quiet, so Pastor Sunti and I thought the family had agreed to do as we told them. I had already spoken to them some weeks before, and now both Ahjon Sunti and I had come again to explain that a man who wants to live in Nam Yawn cannot have two wives. This man knew better, for he is studying with the intention of joining the church. But he kept saying, 'It is our custom. My comrade has died, and I must protect his wife. She will stay with me.' We explained that God has forbidden this to a man who already has a wife, and that if Nam Yawn is God's village, its members must obey Him."

"What did the woman say?" asked Hu.

"She was quite willing to move out of his house. And she said she knew it was wrong, that she had never felt good about living with him, but Meo women do not talk back to their men."

"Yes, that is true."

"We finally told the man that he would have to leave the village if he had set his mind to disobey God. Then his boy spoke up,

'Please, Father, don't make us move. I like it here. I can go to school.' "

"I remember the boy," Hu said, a quick smile lighting his face. "He was a bright student when Ai Sawang and I taught there in the school. But what about the bird cry?"

"Ah, yes. Well, Ahjon Sunti and I thought everyone had finally agreed, because after the strange cry everyone had fallen silent. I see now. The woman must have set her mind even then. Ahjon Sunti and I prayed with them and left, and early the next morning we returned to Chiang Khong. It was only two days later that Ai Sawang appeared in Chiang Khong. He was very agitated and had come to say that the morning we left, the young son had told him how the woman once more pleaded with the man to let her return to her own house, and he again refused. Then they all went to work in the fields. The man did not notice when she left her work. When he arrived home to eat, the fire pit was cold and the woman was dead in her sleeping place. By her side lay a ball of raw opium. You know as well as I how quickly a little piece of it swallowed can put the whole body to sleep—a sleep from which no man can waken another."

"Ah, poor, foolish creature!" Hu cried. "So it goes when people lose their faith. And now what is happening in the village?"

"Ai Sawang tells me there is much bad talk. This husband, who fears the blame of the villagers, is telling the people that I, a Thai, have caused the trouble by meddling in Meo business. Your father, the chief, does not say this of course. He knows what God says, but he is old and the Meo custom is strong on him, so he would not command this man as you would have done had you been there."

"Yes," Hu said sadly, "and you, being a Thai, are at a disadvantage."

"I am most certainly," the pastor sighed. "I really am afraid to go back to Nam Yawn. The Meo people can be very fierce, and——"

"I will go," Hu interrupted. "My teachers will excuse me from my classes. As soon as the special meetings here in Bangkok finish, I will visit the big district pookheng near Houei Sai. Over all the Meo in our place, he is a man of good sense."

DEMON OF PADENG

Some days later Hu and the Thai pastor traveled north by bus to the border town of Chiang Khong, arriving late in the afternoon of the second day at the pastor's home on the bank of the Mekong. The wooden house stood up on posts in typical Thai fashion and had a roofed veranda on the south side. It afforded a fine view of the river, and Ahjon Geo and Hu sat looking at the water and at the town of Houei Sai on the opposite bank. Hu turned from the river to glance back at the lawn and the road from which they had just come. "This is a peaceful place," he remarked.

"Yes," smiled the pastor, "it is to us who are Christians, but you well know, brother, how frightened the spirit worshipers are of this place. I see the local people making obeisance to some unseen power whenever they pass here, but especially in the evening."

"I remember it well," Hu replied, "when I stayed here after we left Nam Tha. The mission got this beautiful site quite cheap because it is a spirit place. Seeing us living here without harm, the local people asked us if they could pasture one or two water buffalo here. We agreed, but one day—I saw it myself—for no reason the buffalo became terrified. I saw it break its rope and run blindly, even passing under the church building, which, as you see, is less than three feet above the ground. The animal was simply mad with fear. Yet we noticed nothing that might have frightened it—not even a dog."

"Yes," agreed the pastor, "and I also have observed such things. But they now pasture the animals here again. They forget the fear because we live here so peacefully."

"It is not enough to defy the spirits," Hu went on almost as if to himself. "We must have faith in God, even as John the friend of the Vatiu Yesu wrote: 'Faith is the victory. It conquers all evil in the world.'"

The two men had been talking so intently that they had not noticed another man approaching until he stood at the foot of the steps leading up to the porch.

"Oh, it is Ai Sawang," the pastor exclaimed, "and with no good news, I would guess, if his face tells me right."

"Yes, I bring more bad news," Ai Sawang answered, his eyes

troubled. "There has been another death."

"Another death," Hu cried. "In Nam Yawn? May God help us."

With a sigh Ai Sawang sat down on a bench near the veranda steps and wiped his round, perspiring face with the back of his hand. "I suppose, Hu, that Ahjon has told you of the woman who died. Since that time much talk has spread around the country, and finally the Lao police in Houei Sai heard of it and sent men to investigate. Someone warned the husband of their approach, and—well, you know how our people fear the police from both Laos and Thailand. With all due respect to you, Ahjon"—Ai Sawang bowed in the direction of the pastor—"it is because both the Thai and the Lao look down on us as ignorant. If anything is wrong, we are always blamed, no matter what——"

"Let us hear the story, Ai Sawang," Hu urged.

"To be sure. Now where was I? Oh, yes. When the man heard the police were coming, he became quite frightened. They asked the neighbors a few questions, but the police had mainly come to escort him to Houei Sai for investigation. Just what they expected to find by taking him there, I don't know. After all, the death took place in Nam Yawn and——"

"What about the death?" Hu interrupted.

"Well, as I was saying, the man was speechless with fear. He expected to be put in prison for many days, I suppose. I don't know. They started to walk him out to the river, and I followed them. As we neared the river the man began to drag his steps. By the time we reached the shore he had fallen on the ground unconscious. 'He has no doubt taken raw opium,' I told them, 'and even like the woman, he will die.'

"The police became very excited then. They called in a fisherman with his motorboat and made him transport us quickly downstream to Houei Sai. But it was too late. By the time we reached the Dooley Clinic the man had died. And now our village is really excited. Before, some people blamed the man who died, but now that he is dead, they accuse Ahjon Geo because he is a Thai. The chief, of course, does not agree with them."

"You see," said Ahjon Geo, throwing up his hands, "it is even worse than what I told you. If I go there now, they will kill me."

"Never mind," Hu urged, his lips set in a firm line. "Tomorrow I will call on the pookheng across the river."

The next day Hu and Ai Sawang crossed the river to Houei Sai and walked to the outer edge of the town where a Meo village sprawled against the mountain. Knowing the rumors of the two suicides had probably reached the ears of the big chief, Hu wondered what their reception would be. The late afternoon shadows stretched across the ground as they approached his large thatched house, and they were pleased when the chief himself, smiling cordially, welcomed them inside. One of his daughters brought out stools and, setting ripe bananas before them on the low wicker table, invited them to rest. Yes, the chief had heard of the tragedies and was indeed sorry for the recent misfortunes.

"The reason I have come," Hu explained, "is that I would like some word from you to take back to my people. You see, while I am studying in Bangkok, a Thai pastor from Chiang Khong has been the spiritual leader over the people in Nam Yawn, and now because he is the one who had to enforce discipline according to God's commands, some blame him for the suicides and threaten him if he returns. As the pookheng, what is your opinion?"

The chief's gaze wandered out past the sunlit vegetable garden at his back door to the hazy line of trees that marked the river. "I know the work of your mission well," he said. "You have strict rules and require the people to change more than any other Christian group. But you help us. I have relatives living in villages near Chiengmai. They have told me of the work of Dr. Lamberton, how he pulls aching teeth and aids the people addicted to opium. This is the kind of assistance we need. Your mission has not forgotten the Meo people, and we are grateful."

"Then you do not blame the Thai pastor for the misfortunes in Nam Yawn?"

"This tragic affair is a family problem," the chief answered gravely. "Tell your people to remember this and to forget trying to put the blame on someone else. If people choose to dwell in a village of the Seven-day mission, then they must keep the rules.

After all, you do not force anyone to live with you."

Thanking the chief, Hu rose, and they parted with mutual respect. The two Meo journeyed to Nam Yawn, where they gathered the people together that same evening and exhorted them with the advice of the chief and the teachings of God. "Let there be no more bad words," Hu said. "If you have chosen to dwell here, then consider well that we live under God's laws. That is why He has protected and blessed the village. If you do not like the laws, no one forces you to stay here. I ask you simply to decide whom you will worship. If you serve the spirits and the old life, that is your choice, but do not stay in Nam Yawn. If you love and honor the great Father in the sky, why then you will be happy here, and you are welcome."

Before he left, Hu was happy to see his younger brother Sua, who had returned after serving in the army. He introduced Hu to his bride, a pretty girl of fourteen, whom he had stolen as the Meo custom allowed, from a nearby Meo village. "We are not baptized yet," the brother explained, "but we have cast out the spirits, and we are studying the Sacred Words and getting ready."

Hu was also happy that the school prospered. Since he had left, a Lao man from the Thai Dom tribe was the teacher. He and his family, refugees from Ahjon Hawn's old church in Nam Tha, had come with several other families that first year.

The next day Hu left, after promising that he would return in December to hold special meetings in the village. On his way to Bangkok he stopped in Chiang Khong to assure Ahjon Geo that he need have no fear of returning to Nam Yawn.

In December, true to his word, Hu returned from school to hold the promised meetings. No one mentioned the past tragedies, and the people, looking forward to hearing the words of God, greeted him gladly. Hu was hopeful and courageous.

The day the meetings would start, Hu went to see the little thatched church he had built with only the children to help him. It was now three years old. A corner sagged where the ground was low in one spot. Inside, the bamboo floor had weakened, making wide cracks between the slats of wood, which sometimes caused the rough benches to tip when sat upon.

DEMON OF PADENG

"We must build a new church on a different site," he mused.

That evening, carrying lanterns, the people gathered at the little church. They sang hymns, and then Hu rose to speak. But he had scarcely begun when there came the sound of hurrying feet. A frightened group appeared at the church door. "Hu, come quickly. It's Sua's wife. She's dying."

Immediately confusion reigned. The people crowded out of the church while Hu, lantern in hand, quickly picked his way among the agitated people. What could be the matter with his brother's girl-bride? Sua came running up beside him. He held his lantern aloft, revealing his wide and frightened eyes.

"She was well just two hours ago," he panted as he ran. "At dusk she went—went to the river to bathe. She said she would —come to the church——"

By now they had arrived at the house. Hu told the crowd to stay back while he and his brother entered. Holding a lantern, two women bent over the corner platform used for sleeping. The dim light fell on a small huddled shape, and as the men drew nearer they could see the girl's pale face, her eyes closed.

One of the women handed Hu an uncapped medicine bottle, which he examined. It had contained antimalaria capsules but was now empty.

"The bottle was almost full yesterday," Sua told Hu. "But what would make her do such a thing?"

"It was because of those Thai Dom," said one of the women, and Hu recognized Lea, Yee's wife. "I know," she continued, "that she has had bad words with them in the past."

Meanwhile Hu took the girl's pulse. "It's weak," he said. "I have no way to empty her stomach, and she is unconscious. All I have is a heart stimulant. Light the fire, Sua." And Hu darted out the door, returning quickly with the little bag he used to carry on his medical trips to the Chiengmai villages. Quickly he boiled a syringe and needle in a pan over the fire. Then he gave the girl an injection of adrenalin, but even as he did, he knew it was too late. Desperately he prayed, but while he held her wrist the feeble pulse faded under his fingers, and she died.

"She breathes no more," Hu said.

With a sob Sua threw himself across the bed weeping. Wails and moans filled the air, and for the first time Hu realized that a crowd had gathered in the house.

Lea still stood numbly with her lantern. "What did you say about words she had with someone?" Hu asked her.

"Oh, yes. Only last week I heard her tell how she had been joking with the Thai Dom girls. She was teasing them because they are not married. Said one of them should marry you, Hu, because you are past twenty-five, too old to be single. But those girls sneered and said, 'We are Lao. We would never marry a Meo. You mountain people are ignorant.' She cried when she told about it, for she was greatly hurt. 'We mountain people are better than those lazy lowland people,' she said. 'If they speak to me like this again, I will kill myself.' " Lea shook her head in bewilderment. "I thought no more of her threat. But it seems—it seems her mind——"

"Do any of the rest of you know about this?" Hu addressed the crowd.

"Yes, yes," chorused several voices. "What Lea says is true."

Hu searched the faces revealed by the light of his lantern. "Has anyone questioned the Lao girls?"

"I asked them what they knew," one boy called out, "and all they say is that they were joking, and she became angry for nothing."

"Well," sighed Hu, "what is done, is done. The girl has taken her life. That is clear. Stirring up further blame will not bring back the dead. Let us have no quarreling over this tragedy. We have sadness enough. Now, go home quietly and we will prepare for a Christian burial."

The next day they wrapped the girl in cloth and bore the body out to the edge of the village. The family wailed and mourned as was their custom, but there was no khene or drums, no squealing of pigs or blood of oxen. The people listened as Hu read from the Sacred Words of how Vatiu Yesu is the resurrection and the life, and the sobbing subsided as the believers sang hymns of hope around the grave.

DEMON OF PADENG

Finally, three days after the time originally planned, the chastened villagers gathered again for the promised revival meetings. Translating from the Thai, Hu read to them from Paul's letter to the Ephesians. " 'Our fight is not with flesh and blood, but with spirit beings of power, with those who control the dark things of this world, and with the evil spirits of the air. . . . You must take faith as your shield.'

"You remember," he reminded them, "how Ahjon Wick, on his first visit to our village, warned us that though by faith we had conquered the spirits, we must not think we are beyond the danger of evil. Whenever we lose faith, we do wrong, and we open the way for the enemy to harm us.

"The three who have died here so needlessly, so foolishly, did so because they lost sight of the Father in the sky and of His strength and His wisdom. They looked on things as the enemy commanded their minds, and they lost their faith. Nothing is so dangerous as to lose faith and let the enemy put his darkness upon us.

"God has not left us. His promises are still bright and strong. Let us keep them before us, for He says, 'I am with you for untold future days, even to the end of the world.' "

A few days later, Hu called to his brothers as well as several other young men, "It is time to build a new house for God. The old one is rotting and fallen." They walked between the houses and decided on a level, well-drained area near the entrance to the village.

"First, let us take down the old building," Hu directed. "It looks bad in the village, and besides, the foundation posts are still good. I cut them myself. They are decay-resistant, and we can use them again."

Pulling down the rotting thatch and the termite-ridden bamboo took but a short while, and soon they had everything stripped down to the old floor. The sagging bamboo slats they quickly pulled apart, and the tall posts of donyong that Hu had brought with such labor three years before were as strong as ever. Several men stepped forward, lifting the first post out of the ground.

"That won't be necessary," Hu said, approaching them. "I carried them by myself when I built this. You men were in the army then." And so he reached for the log they held upright, intending to heave it to his shoulder. To his utter surprise he succeeded only in pushing it over. It fell to the ground with a resounding thud, heavy as granite.

The men all burst out laughing. "Hu thinks he is an elephant," his brother chuckled. "No man carries donyong alone. Anyone knows that."

Standing in blank amazement, Hu scarcely heard their laughter or their teasing. "Laugh as you like," he said at last, "but God is my witness. Three years ago I did carry each of these logs by myself, all twelve of them. I was alone. There was no other way. The good Father, knowing my need, sent me strength." Then Hu recounted the details of his experience.

The men stopped laughing, hushed by his words. They did not doubt him. There had been a need. He had prayed, and God had answered.

And now he prayed again: "Great Father in the sky, we are weak, but You are strong, and always You remember us. Thank You for Your love, faithful like the sun, clear like the rain. Help us not to forget You."

So the men, encouraged by remembering God's goodness, worked together to carry the heavy posts, cut the bamboo, and gather rattan so that they finished the new church in a few days.

Chapter 5

TRIAL OF FAITH

It was the third morning that someone had spotted the tiger tracks. Though the footprints never wandered far from the river, each day they came closer to the edge of the village. "Father thinks this fellow is after his goats," Yee commented as he examined the fresh prints that edged the pool where he stood with Hu.

"I think he is right," Hu answered, "but some of the villagers grow fearful, especially Niu Sae Chang's wife. They have only just burned the spirits and have not yet learned fully to trust God."

"Yes," said Yee, "I noticed the other day how pale her baby looked as she carried him on her back. He has malaria, I suppose."

"Yes, it is malaria, and I took her some medicine. The child gets better, but the old beliefs are strong. These tiger tracks bring back all the old fears. You know all those stories of the tiger spirit women that come at night bringing death. The old way to deal with it would be to call the tu-ua-neng to carry on the incantations and make the sacrifices with all the tiresome old customs."

"Tiresome and costly," Yee agreed. "But we are Christians, and what will we do?"

"Why, we'll shoot the tiger," Hu laughed. "One good bullet from my big rifle and neither goats nor people need fear him again."

"Good." Yee grinned. "Shall we try tonight?"

"Tonight. May the Lord give me a straight eye." Hu paused to take in the curve of the bank, the distance from tree to river, the thick clump of bamboo close to the water. "We'll meet here a little while before sunset. That is the time when Pookheng Tiger comes to drink."

"That tiger is as good as dead," Yee chuckled, rubbing his hands together.

"I'll be going back to Bangkok in a few days," Hu mused, "and a thick tiger skin should bring a good price. I need all the money I can find."

Hu had always been the most thrifty of all the brothers; so Yee showed no surprise when he talked of saving his money. "Could it be," Yee added mischievously, "that you are saving for a bride price?"

"Who knows?" Hu murmured, avoiding his brother's eyes. "A man cannot go single all his life."

Yee glanced sharply at his brother, who gazed with a dreamy expression at the trees across the river. "But who will it be?" Yee persisted. "The girls in the village are only children—or foreigners," he added dourly. "Will you follow the Meo custom and steal a girl from some other village? She would be a spirit worshiper, of course."

"What law says she must be a Meo?"

Although the brother's face showed his surprise, he asked no further questions, for they were approaching the outer houses of the village. At that moment children came running up shouting, "The tiger, the tiger! Are you going to shoot it, Uncle Hu?"

Great excitement pervaded the village when Hu announced his plan, but he gave specific commands that only those invited to the hunt would help him.

Two hours before sunset Hu gathered a half dozen of the best marksmen, with their guns. He stationed them well hidden some distance back from the pool where he expected the tiger to drink. Then he and his brother Yee, stepping noiselessly, hid themselves among the bamboo downwind of the tiger's anticipated path and waited.

Tensely they listened for the slightest noise. The mottled sunlight on the path faded. Overhead the sky reddened, and the wind rustled the papery leaves. Then suddenly they felt, more than heard, a presence. Hu heard his brother's quickened breath and felt his own heart pounding in his throat. A great striped shape glided along the path and stooped to the water. Raising his rifle, Hu watched the animal through his gunsight. There came the liquid sound of wrinkling water as the tiger lapped. Then almost as though he sensed them, the great beast lifted its head to look with huge yellow eyes in the direction of their hiding place. Hu waited no longer. Taking aim, he pulled the trigger. The blast shook the leaves. With a terrible yowl, the tiger sprang into the air, loped a few feet, and fell to the ground.

The two men waited tensely, watching the great tawny body where it lay on the path.

"You got him," Yee whispered.

"Yes, I think so, with just one shot."

"There is seldom a second shot with a tiger."

Cautiously they approached the motionless animal. Hu poked the haunches with his rifle. "Thank God," he said. "I hardly expected to do it. The light was dim. What a beautiful coat he has!"

With shouts and laughter the other men raced toward him. "A great shot, Hu," they cried.

Last of all came Yang Si, the father. "Well, perhaps the goats will be safe now," he said.

"Yes," Hu added, "and our people will know that they need not fear any tiger spirit and the death it brings."

Three days later Hu was riding the bus, headed for Bangkok. The tiger skin, carefully rolled and wrapped in cloth, gave him great satisfaction. "I should get a good price," he gloated. "Let's see, I will soon have ten thousand *baht*. That's almost five hundred American dollars. Many people would be quite surprised if they knew why I am saving. Well, they will find out soon enough."

Hu glanced at his watch—not so much to see the time as to feel the satisfaction of owning such a timepiece. In Nam Yawn he scarcely thought of it or used it, but now on his way back to Bangkok his mind began to fall into the habits that world required. He had become accustomed to the adjustment from primitive village to big city, slipping into the patterns of the one or the other as required.

It was good to return to school. He loved his classes, for learning had been a passion with him since first he began to read in the little school in Nam Tha. And he couldn't wait to see his roommate, Rangsit. They had been friends since Nam Tha days. In Bangkok, Rangsit was the only other Meo that he saw often. He would be interested in the tiger hunt. Hu's eyes kindled as he anticipated telling him the story. "Only one shot, Rangsit. And the light was not good."

He wondered if he would have the chance to tell Kaifah about the tiger. Probably not. The thought of having such a long conversation with *her* made his heart race. Smiling to himself, he mused about how no one—not his family or Rangsit or Ahjon Wick—knew about his feelings for Kaifah. Except perhaps Kaifah. Yes, she probably knew. A light glowed in her eyes when she smiled at him. "Father in the sky," he prayed, "if it is in Your plan, please bless my dream, and help me to save the money I need."

Sometimes he allowed himself to wonder how much the bride price would be for a Thai girl. He had heard Thai men discussing the subject. Sometimes they mentioned five thousand baht or even ten thousand. Because he was a Meo, the girl's family would probably want more—that is, if they even considered him at all. He sighed deeply. Oh, he must save and save. Already he had two silver neck rings worth ten thousand baht, but he would not use them for the bride price—he wanted to keep them for a special gift to Kaifah. He thought of them with satisfaction, wrapped in cloth and laid on the top shelf of the locker by the door of his room. On the second shelf sat his radio and camera. Not many Meo had such things. By saving every penny from his mission allowance and growing his own food in a little garden he had managed to buy them, for he felt that people would expect a mountain tribesman who wanted to marry a Thai girl to have fine possessions.

Now the bus passed through the outlying reaches of the city. The street followed a canal which became dirtier as they progressed into the city. Hu watched a fisherman with a great net stretched over a framework like a huge umbrella. It was slowly lowered into the water by a long pole fastened to a wooden platform. The fisherman lifted the net as the bus passed, and Hu could see how few and small were the fish he had caught. The mountain tribesman smiled, remembering the fat, silver fish in the Nam Yawn River, and wondered if Kaifah would ever see the place and if she would love his village as much as he did.

The traffic thickened as they approached the central city. Buses filled the streets. School children swarmed on them, some hanging precariously to the outside. Between the roaring trucks and automobiles, three-wheeled bicycles, each with a sidecar holding a passenger, threaded a dangerous path. Hu decided he would never want to drive such a vehicle, for both driver and passenger were continually vulnerable to the crush of the traffic. "Let me rather lead my little packhorse on a mountain trail, no matter how narrow it is," he told himself.

The bus at last made its way to the central depot, and Hu, gathering up his bundles, quickly picked his way among the people with their baskets of yams, pineapple, and coconuts, the wicker cages full of chirping birds and chickens, the hawkers with their food carts, frying noodles and garlic, prawns and chicken.

Soon he caught a bus to the mission compound and disembarked at the road. After the confusion and heat of the city, he felt thankful for the peace of lawns and shade trees. He hurried along to the press building, where he lived in one of the back rooms with the other ministerial students. Just ahead of him he saw a man open the door and enter. Though the daylight was fading, he recognized Rangsit. Good! He would be able to show him the tiger skin.

In the next few days Hu got back into the routine of work and classes and managed to find time to take his tiger skin into the city to a merchant who gave him six hundred baht for it. As always he set aside his tithe and put the rest in an envelope, laying it on the shelf in his locker beside his camera and radio.

Sabbath came, and he and Rangsit, with the other students, went to Sabbath School and church service. After eating at the school cafeteria, they returned to their room for a minute. Hu needed a book for a Bible study he planned to attend. As they stepped into the room, Rangsit asked, "Did you leave your locker open?"

"No, I never do," Hu said, stepping over to investigate. Then he saw that the second shelf was empty. His camera, radio, and the envelope of money were gone. Quickly he searched the lower shelves and the floor. "Rangsit," he cried, "I have been robbed!"

"What!" exclaimed Rangsit. "Are your silver neck rings gone too?"

Hu felt along the highest shelf. "No, they're still here. But who could have taken my other things?" He stood stunned a minute, his mind whirling. Then he reached up to the top shelf and brought down the cloth-wrapped bundle. "Thieves, here in this place. Nothing is safe anywhere. I will take this silver to Ahjon Wick now before someone steals it as well."

He started out the door, and Rangsit followed him. Shocked and angry, Hu exploded, "What a fool I was to leave anything valuable in a locker! But of course I am here with God's people. I thought I was safe." The young men followed the walk that divided the compound and led to the pastor's house. "I have been robbed, Rangsit, robbed! Do you hear? A thief among Christians! God's people!" The last phrase he uttered with withering contempt.

Rangsit gave him a sidelong glance full of hurt astonishment. "I've never heard you talk like this before," he said. "Hu, you must remember——"

"I've never been robbed before," Hu snapped, clutching his silver and walking so fast that Rangsit had to run a little to keep up.

By then they had reached the house of the mission president, who welcomed them kindly and listened to Hu's story. "But only think, Ahjon. A thief on the mission compound! Here I am living among God's people, and I am robbed. I don't understand. This cannot be God's place, or His people, if they do things like this."

"Hu, I know this is a great loss to you," the pastor said, "but let's be thankful that the thief didn't take your neck rings. That would have been a much greater loss. Come, we will put your silver in the vault at the mission office. It will be safe there."

The pastor led them out of the house and across the compound to the office building while Hu continued lamenting bitterly, "I don't understand it, Ahjon. This would not happen in a Meo village, even a heathen one. The spirit worshipers teach their children never to steal, and the villages strictly enforce the law. But here I am among Christians, and——"

DEMON OF PADENG

"Yes, Hu, I know the Meo are strictly honest, but you are in Thailand in a big city. Thievery is common here. Many people think nothing of it, because they don't know God's law, and the city cannot enforce the law as well as in a Meo village. Remember, too, that even on this compound many people come and go who are neither Christians nor members of the church."

Hu ignored the older man. "But, Ahjon," he persisted, "I have put myself in God's hands and asked Him to protect me, and what has happened? He didn't hear. Maybe He doesn't care about me."

For the moment the pastor said no more. They had arrived at the mission office building, and he led the way to the room which housed the vault. Finding a large brown envelope, he put the silver neck rings in it, sealed it, and wrote Hu's name on the outside. Only when he had locked the package in the vault did he turn to face the Meo student. Putting his hand on his shoulder, he said gravely, "Hu, these doubts that are attacking your mind do not come from God, but from the enemy. Beware. You have lost some material possessions, but the enemy wants to steal something more precious, and that is your faith."

Rangsit, who had been standing numbly by, suddenly burst out, "I don't know what is wrong with you, Hu. I've never heard you talk this way before."

"And I tell you I've never been robbed before." His voice was sullen. "I'm not sure what I will do. What good is it to be a Christian? I thought God cared for His children. Maybe I'm not in the right place."

The three passed through the empty building in silence and went out. The pastor paused to lock the door while Hu paced back and forth on the sidewalk in front of the door. "I don't know what to do. Maybe I will take my things and go back to my village. The Meo do not steal." With that, he turned on his heel and started back to his room, followed by a bewildered Rangsit.

"I'm not going anywhere today," Hu told him. "If you want to go to the Bible study, you can." And he went into his room, threw himself onto his bunk, and lay there brooding.

For a long time he watched a big fly buzzing endlessly as it bumped against the window screen trying to find a way out. It reminded Hu of his own frustration. "Why," he fretted, "why did God let it happen to me?" It wasn't so much the things themselves, though he was sorry to lose them, of course. But he felt angry toward God. How could He allow wicked people to treat him so? "I thought You always cared for Your children," he grumbled. "You know what I'm saving for. You're the only one I've told. And I especially asked You to help me save for—for Kaifah." He closed his aching eyes as the slow tears wet his cheeks.

Then from somewhere a saner voice spoke in his mind. "Who, do you think, helped you kill the tiger? Things could have been different, you know. The tiger might have killed you. Only last week you learned how I helped you. Only a small thing, perhaps. But you needed to carry some logs to build a church once, remember? And look at all the spirit places where you have stayed. Never has the enemy touched you, and there have been people healed——"

By now Hu's tears fell fast as he buried his face in his pillow. "Yes, yes, Father, You have cared for me," he sobbed, "but why didn't You this time? Why? Why?"

He heard a step in the hall, and quickly wiping his face on his blanket, sat up as Rangsit came in. "Oh, you are still here, Ai Hu. It's getting dark," he said as he switched on the light. "I've been talking to the other students in the building. We've all decided to pray especially about your problem. And we're going to watch, too, to see if we can find the thief. I believe God will help us."

Rangsit spoke with such eagerness and interest in his face that Hu felt a little ashamed. "Thank you, Rangsit."

Hu rose and started for the door. "I'm going for a walk," he said, and went out. The blackness of the night matched the gloom of his soul. Yes, it was true, God sometimes did good things for him, but at other times He didn't seem to be around. Thieves got past the good angels, it seemed. Hu walked round the compound, his hands in his pockets, his head lowered. The more he listened to the dark thoughts, the more discouraged he became. Was God, after all, so different from the spirits he had once worshiped? He was strong, to be sure, but what good was His power if the enemy still could reach Christians to hurt them?

Once again he circled the compound. At one point he almost went into Ahjon Wick's house, but thought better of it. No. It was no use to disturb the man. Hu Sae Yang would make up his own mind. He turned toward his room, having decided what he would do. In a few days he would gather his things and return home. What use was it to be a pastor? He could grow rice and catch fish and live out his days on the soil like the rest of his people. It would be hard to leave Kaifah, of course. That thought choked him. Blinking back the tears, he entered his room. Rangsit was already asleep, so Hu undressed in the dark and crept into his bunk without even kneeling to pray as he usually did.

The next morning he rose woodenly, his eyes burning and his head aching. Mechanically he dressed and ate and went to his classes, saying little to anyone. He considered himself quite forsaken by God. As he hurried across the lawn, head bent, he suddenly bumped into someone. Looking up, he recognized Ahjon Dybdahl, a young American pastor whom he felt especially close to since he was the only American he knew who was acquainted with the Meo language. *Zia Cha,* honorable elder, the Meo people around Chiengmai had called him.

"Oh, it is you, Zia Cha."

"I've heard about your misfortune," the pastor said in Meo. "I am sorry about it, Hu."

"Yes, well . . ." Hu shrugged. "These things happen to everyone alike, Christian and heathen. It matters little to God, I guess. Sometimes He helps us, but other times He looks elsewhere. The spirits are the same. I am going home to Nam Yawn, I think." Hu had been gazing off into the distance as he spoke. Now he glanced at the pastor, and the grave concern in the blue eyes caught at his own.

"Hu," the man said, "did you never think of a better reason why God allowed someone to touch your treasure?"

Something in the kind voice made Hu ashamed, and he looked down at his feet.

"I know, Hu, that you are careful with money. You have managed to save a good sum, probably more than any other student. That money meant a lot to you. Perhaps it meant too much. Long ago Vatiu warned, 'Do not store treasure on earth where thieves can steal it. But rather store treasure in heaven where it is safe, for your heart will be where your treasure is.' Perhaps your possessions held too much of your heart. Think about it, Hu."

The mountain youth felt close to tears as the pastor went on his way, but he could not deny his wisdom. All the rest of the day he kept thinking of the words, "Perhaps your possessions held too much of your heart."

The next day he searched out Ahjon Wick. "Ahjon," he began, "Zia Cha thinks that maybe God is testing me because I was beginning to love money too much. What do you think?"

"Hu," the pastor said, "God has never promised to keep us from all trouble. On this earth we find ourselves in a battle. For the present we live in enemy territory; so we can expect to get wounded sometimes. God allows our faith to be tested so that we may learn *He* is our greatest treasure."

"But I've given myself to God, and I am doing His work."

"Of course you are, but faith is most important. The Lord doesn't want us to worship Him because He saves us from all trouble. That would be a poor reason. We follow Him because He is right and good and because He loved us first. The apostle said that the test of our faith teaches endurance."

Hu looked thoughtful a moment. Then something like a smile lighted his face. "Ahjon, the boys are praying that we will find the thief. Should we pray for this?"

"Yes, I think so. When we have endured the test, sometimes God returns our possessions. He did for Job. If the thief is one of our trusted students, we certainly want to know it now. Whoever he is, we can try to get back your things. That will surely require God's help. In this country hardly anyone ever recovers anything stolen. The thieves take things to the pawnshops so that lost articles are almost impossible to trace. But God can help us find your things if it is His will."

DEMON OF PADENG

Some days later Hu appeared again at the pastor's office. "Ahjon," he said, "the boys have been praying and asking people, and they think they know who the thief is. They believe it may be that fellow who cleans the presses. He works near our rooms and knows the place well. Since he is not a believer, he was not in church Sabbath, but he knows we are gone then. Someone saw him near our door in the morning while we were gone to church."

The pastor looked grave. "The other mission workers and I have also been praying. While I want to take care not to accuse anyone falsely, I will make inquiries about the man, and if it appears best, I'll talk to him myself."

A few days later the pastor called Hu into his office. "I asked the students you told me about," he began, "and I decided on their testimony to call the suspected man in. I prayed much about it, for seldom does anyone make a thief confess, at least in this city. But after I confronted him with the evidence, he finally admitted taking the radio. He said it was in a certain pawnshop, and he produced the ticket. I sent him to buy it back, and he did." The pastor opened his desk drawer and produced the missing radio.

Hu received it with a big smile and, after examining it, said, "It seems to be in good condition. Thank you, Ahjon."

"About the camera and the money," the pastor continued, "he insists he knows nothing, but since he took the radio, I find it hard to believe him."

"We will keep praying, Ahjon," Hu said with something like his old confidence, and he went out quickly, not wanting the pastor to see the tears gathering in his eyes. A flood of emotions swelled in his mind, feelings of joy and sadness, contrition and pride—joy at the returned radio with its evidence of God's care but sadness and contrition as he remembered his stormy rebellion and doubt of God. Through it all he felt proud of his Christian brothers who had never lost interest in his case but had continued in prayer for him. "Dear Father in the sky," he prayed, "You have been good to me who sinned against You. I am sorry I doubted You, because I see You are good, and Your love endures always."

More than a week later Pastor Wick called Hu again. "Another miracle has happened," he smiled. "I continued making inquiries about the man who took your radio. Because of things he had said, his fellow workers were all sure he had taken your other things; so I talked to him again, and he finally confessed that he had stolen the camera and the cash. He told me he had given the pawn ticket to a friend who lives up country, but he promised to get it back. I called in the press manager, too, and he has agreed to deduct a sum from the man's wages every week until he has paid back the money he owes you. Hu, I call it a miracle. There was no reason why he should have admitted it to me. I had no airtight case. He could have kept on denying his guilt forever, and we would have been helpless."

Hu had been listening with bowed head. Then he looked up, a shy smile on his face. "I was only thinking, Ahjon, that the Lord is better to me than I deserve. I know we'll get the camera back too."

And Hu's restored faith had its reward. It took three months for the thief to get the pawn ticket back from his friend, but finally one day Ahjon Wick presented Hu with the camera. By then the man had paid back the money also.

"Well, Hu, what do you think now?" the pastor asked him.

"I was a fool, Ahjon, and yet how patient is our God. He reminded me of His past interest and protection and kept my Christian brothers praying for me. I know now as never before that God really cares about me. It is even as you said, Ahjon. When God tests our faith, we learn endurance, and that is of more value than radios or cameras or many baht."

DEMON OF PADENG

Chapter 6

KAIFAH

"Is it true that Kaifah will be leaving soon? I thought I heard you mention something yesterday." Hu tried to sound matter-of-fact, but his Thai friend Prasan laughed.

"Don't fear, Hu. I know your heart." They stopped by a low stone wall, and Prasan set his books down. "It is like this," he said. "My mother has come here to Bangkok for surgery in the mission hospital. When she is ready to go home to Ubon, Kaifah will go too. The girl hasn't been home for a while, so she will be glad to go with her grandmother on the bus."

"When will she go?" Hu's voice was anxious in spite of himself.

Prasan flicked a twig at a chameleon that scurried along the wall. "My mother will not be ready to travel immediately. Probably in about two weeks. I'll be going, too, since we'll have a holiday from school then. I'll travel on my motorcycle."

By now Hu was only half listening. A wild thought had come into his head, and he hardly dared speak of it. Yet, why not? The other student was his friend, wasn't he? Finally he blurted out, "Prasan, what would happen——? Do you think Kaifah——? Well, I mean—I want to go with you."

Laughing good-naturedly, Prasan replied, "The best thing to do is to ask Kaifah. If she is willing for you to come——" He shrugged and picked up his books. "You can ride with me on my motorcycle."

His heart pounding, his mind in a whirl, Hu went on his way. Should he be bold enough to ask Kaifah such a thing? She occupied his thoughts so much that to him it seemed natural to be with her as much as possible. Sometimes he believed she knew how he felt about her, but at other times he wondered.

Hu smiled, remembering the first time he had met Kaifah. He had stopped by Prasan's apartment to get some notes from a class he had missed. Somewhere in the back of the apartment a baby cried. Then the wail had stopped. Presently a girl came into the room carrying Prasan's small son. With a plain white blouse and a simple cotton *pahsin* wrapped about her like a skirt, she might have been a servant. But her serenely lovely face instantly attracted Hu.

"I will be taking the child out walking, Uncle," she told him. "I will be back soon." Her voice was soft.

Prasan glanced up. "Fine, Kaifah. Hu, this is my niece who has come to care for the baby. My wife must work at the hospital at night, you know."

With a shy smile the girl bowed in Hu's direction, her lashes touching her cheeks as she lowered her gaze. Then she turned to go. Hu had just a glimpse of a dark knot of hair against a slender neck before the door closed.

"She arrived just last week," Prasan commented. "She has been a great help for us, I assure you. Now about those notes, the professor explained that——"

Hu scarcely listened. He wondered how Prasan could sit there so matter-of-factly talking of school and work. With a great effort he brought his attention to the business at hand, but he determined to know Kaifah. From then on he found occasion to seek help from Prasan often. His need was not altogether feigned, for he was attending school in Thai, a foreign language, and Prasan was Thai.

But Hu's main subject of study was Kaifah. Like most Oriental girls, she was shy and retiring in the presence of men not of her family. She looked delicate, but worked steadily, even strenuously. Always moving quietly in the background, she placed dishes on the table, cut and arranged flowers, prepared the food in the kitchen, but most often she carried and comforted the child.

One night Prasan and Hu returned late from a meeting in a distant village. "Stay here," Prasan suggested. "There is no sense in waking your roommate at this hour."

DEMON OF PADENG

"Wait, I will fix you a bed," Kaifah said with her usual quiet faithfulness. Soon she returned with something that appeared to be bed coverings. Hu noticed their whiteness. She spread them on the low couch by the wall for him.

During the night he became conscious of the baby crying. Once he looked up and caught a glimpse of Kaifah as she passed under the dim light in the hall. "She cares for the child even in the night," he thought, "yet she is not its mother. I've never heard her raise her voice in complaint as many women would." Increasingly Hu concluded that Kaifah was the girl he wanted to marry, but always in his heart he added, "If it is what pleases You, Father in the sky."

And now came the marvelous but frightening idea that he ask Kaifah if he could go home with her for a visit. One moment it seemed a natural request that she would smilingly grant. The next he wondered how he could be so foolish as to think this beautiful Thai girl would look at him at all. She lived in an American-style house with store furniture and white bed coverings and a fine bathing place with water in a faucet and tiles on the floor. Hu was very conscious that he came from a primitive village of bamboo huts with floors of earth. At such thoughts his heart turned into a knot of darkness, and tears stung his eyes. "O Father in the sky, help me to keep believing in Your plan. You will guide me."

By now he stood at the door of Prasan's small apartment. As he hesitated, the door opened and Kaifah came out carrying the baby. The sun gleamed on her smooth, black hair as she smiled and greeted him politely. She turned down the path and had started walking quickly away from him before Hu finally found his tongue.

"Kaifah," he called, but his voice was only a whisper. Angry with himself for the way his voice had failed, he cleared his throat. "Kaifah." The name was more of a croak than the well-modulated tone he wanted, but the girl turned, a little smile playing around her mouth. Did he detect a glint of amusement in her eyes? He plunged on desperately. "Kaifah," he said, striding over to her. "I understand—that is—well, Prasan said you might be going home with your grandmother, and well, I—I would like to go with you." In confusion Hu stopped and looked at his feet.

Her bright eyes concentrated on his face while the child in her arms wriggled, prattled, and patted her cheek. When Hu paused, she smiled. "Of course, Ai Hu, I think it would be nice if you came with us. Grandmother and I would be glad for your help. It's a long journey—a full day on the bus."

Hu felt dizzy with relief and delight. "Oh, thank you, Kaifah, thank you!" he exclaimed, and not able to think of anything more to say, he fled, his feelings a mixture of great joy at her answer and self-reproach at his own awkwardness.

Two weeks passed quickly, for school kept Hu greatly occupied, but thoughts of the coming journey filled his mind in spare moments. Some days he abandoned himself to happy expectation, and on others he decided that surely she would have no reason to want him to go with her, and probably she had only been joking when she agreed for him to come. Once as Hu walked by the apartment house he saw Kaifah on the lawn with the baby. She set the child down to play on the grass, and running over to him asked, "Do you still want to come home with me when I go with my grandmother?"

"Oh, yes, yes. My mind has not changed at all."

"That is good. We will leave on the early bus from the depot in the city at four thirty next Wednesday morning. Will that be possible for you?"

"I will be there."

The journey on the bus might have been tedious to others, but to Hu it was highest happiness. As soon as she found a seat the little grandmother had leaned her head against the bus window and fallen into a doze. For the first time since they had met, Hu and Kaifah had a chance for uninterrupted conversation. The couple sat in awkward silence at first until Kaifah said, "Hu, I've heard Prasan say that you live in a Christian village and you started it. Tell me how it began."

Gladly Hu launched into the story of Nam Yawn, telling of the curse of Padeng and of the courage of the few who believed enough in the power of the Father in the sky that they braved the warnings of neighbors and their own fears to settle in the forbidden place. And there they had planted rice and it had wonderfully prospered;

so they had built permanent houses, knowing God was with them. He related how after that more families came and how the village grew more and more renowned in that country as travelers carried word of its success and the greatness of the God of Nam Yawn.

"Because the rice has always grown so well," Hu went on, "we decided to build water mills to thresh it. The women couldn't keep up with the work, using the old way. You know, even here, you tread on the log hammer that pounds the hulls from the rice."

"Oh, yes," Kaifah said, "I have done it myself. It is quite wearisome."

"My father is the chief of Nam Yawn, and he suggested that we make wheels like the Thai Dom people did in Nam Tha. So some of the men thought they remembered how, and they did make a wheel of bamboo with woven matting for the paddles. They could then thresh from morning till night, for the river never wearies of turning the wheel that makes the hammer rise and fall. The people were so happy about it that they made more. Of course they must make new ones after each rainy season because the river rises and carries the old wheels away."

Kaifah had listened attentively. "I have never seen such a device," she said. "I would like to see the ones you speak of."

"Oh, you must see them," Hu answered eagerly, feeling that the conversation was taking a most profitable turn. "You must come to visit Nam Yawn sometime. I have many things to show you there."

The bus stopped then, and Kaifah moved across the aisle to share her grandmother's seat so that no stranger would separate her from them. But Hu and Kaifah still visited across the aisle. Around noon Kaifah produced packages of sticky rice wrapped in banana leaves and some cold chicken. They had bananas and tangerines as well, and Hu thought he had never tasted food so delicious. The grandmother woke to eat and smiled a toothless smile at Hu. "This is a nice boy you have brought, Kaifah. He helps with our bundles, and he likes to eat." And she cackled a dry little chuckle.

During the afternoon Hu told Kaifah of the repeated flights from the insurgents and of his days in the school at Nam Tha. The afternoon sped by. Suddenly Kaifah announced that the next stop would be Ubon. Hu looked at his watch and saw with surprise that the time was four thirty.

Arriving at the city, Hu helped the grandmother down from the bus and carried out the bundles. Kaifah set down her suitcase. "It seems that my uncle Prasan has not arrived yet." She looked perplexed but only for a minute. "Well, never fear. We will take grandmother to my cousin's place. She lives on the edge of town. Prasan will come later, and we will go to my father's house tomorrow."

So saying, she signaled to the driver of one of the many rickshas that thronged about the station, and he cycled over, his car rattling behind him. The women went in his car, and Hu and the luggage with another driver. Soon they left the city behind, and as they rode along the irrigation canals they could see the golden rice paddies stretching into the distance, for it would soon be harvesttime. The cousin's place was a typical Thai country house that sat on posts on a green knoll in the midst of a paddy field. The travelers were glad to find a place to set down their luggage and rest. Kaifah's cousin, a round-faced peasant woman, welcomed them warmly and served them cool water and slices of pineapple. Then she led the grandmother to a back room to rest. Presently the cousin excused herself to go on an errand, leaving Hu and Kaifah sitting in the front room of the house looking at each other.

"Grandmother is resting," Kaifah said, "and it is much more pleasant outside. Let us go walking." She started for the door, and Hu happily followed her. They took the main road for a short way, then turned down a path that followed the irrigation ditch. "I used to like walking by this *klong* when I was a little girl," Kaifah said. Picking a bright red hibiscus, she tossed it into the water. Only then did they notice the large water buffalo almost completely submerged in the water. He snorted as the flower floated toward him, and Kaifah laughed like a child. "That makes me think of how I used to ride on a buffalo as a child. Sometimes my brother would go with me." She chattered on about some of the happy times of her girlhood.

DEMON OF PADENG

Hu had never heard her talk so much before, certainly not about herself, nor had he ever seen her so carefree. "How old are you, Kaifah?" he asked, then trembled inwardly at his daring.

"I am twenty-one years old. You are twenty-eight, I think, aren't you?"

Hu nodded, pleased that she knew.

"You seem older than that to me, and so very serious," she said, "but after today I know why, now that you have told me of all the trouble and of the many times you've had to flee from your home and start all over again."

"But only think, Kaifah, if I had remained in Nam Chuiy I would never have become a Christian. I would never have known how good is the Father in the sky. Living in Nam Yawn has taught me so much about Him and Vatiu Yesu."

They had reached a big mango tree that spread its shade on the path and over the clear water of the klong. Together they sat down in the shadow. "Nam Yawn," repeated Kaifah. "The more you talk about it, the more I am interested. Maybe I will visit that place someday."

Wanting to be sure she would understand his next words, Hu looked at her, but Kaifah was gazing down the length of the klong at a long-legged water bird that seemed to be fishing for frogs.

"Do you really want to see Nam Yawn?" he asked, and not waiting for her answer, he went on. "Kaifah, you are Thai and I am Meo. There are many differences, but if I should ask your parents for you, and they agreed, would you marry me? Would you be willing to go back with me and live in Nam Yawn? To me it is a special village, but I know that to a Thai it is only, well, a little country village far up in Laos——" His words hung unfinished in the air.

When he had begun to speak, Kaifah had turned to glance at him but had quickly lowered her eyes under the intentness of his gaze. As he finished speaking she stared in the direction of the long-legged water bird again, but she didn't see it. "I'll be happy to go with you to Nam Yawn," she replied, "if my parents will let me."

As they walked back to the house they were quieter than they had been. Hu wondered, "Does she really mean she will marry me?

She said only that she would travel to Nam Yawn with me. Maybe she had in mind only for a visit." But he had begun to hope and now feared to question further lest that frail hope be destroyed.

That night they stayed with the cousin, who fixed Hu a bed under a mosquito net on the wide front porch, and the next morning they hired a ricksha and went to Kaifah's village to meet her family. They found that Prasan had arrived and had had a good visit with Kaifah's parents already. Hu was pleased with the warmth of the welcome he received, both from Kaifah's energetic, talkative father and from her mother. A quiet woman like Kaifah, she moved softly in the background always righting this or settling that, hushing a child or bringing food and drink, the unobtrusive center of the family. The father left for his work in the village. The mother busied herself in and out of the house. Several children continually came and went, and Kaifah took up various chores. Hu enjoyed watching her work. He followed her to the cookhouse and was glad to see that it had only an earthen floor. Perhaps she wouldn't find Nam Yawn houses so different after all.

He watched her chopping the green onions she had brought in from the garden, her small deft hands moving with skill and grace. She looked up with a laugh. "My mother told me that Prasan has already been telling them about you."

"Yes?"

"Oh, yes. Prasan says you are a fine young man, that you are very industrious and know well how to handle money."

"Was that all?"

"Oh, I don't know," Kaifah answered, blushing, and she quickly turned to the stove where the oil in the black iron pan had begun to smoke. Tossing in the vegetables she stirred them so vigorously that Hu knew she would say no more.

He noted that a kind of molded cement box enclosed the cook fire. It had openings in the top to heat at least two pots at one time. "That's a very fine firebox," he said. "In Nam Yawn we just build our fires on the earth. It is the Meo custom."

"But I think it would be possible to bring a stove such as this to Nam Yawn," she replied.

DEMON OF PADENG

The evening passed with supper and an hour or two of family visiting. Hu received a bed on the front porch, where Kaifah fastened up his mosquito net over his straw mat. Then she bade him goodnight. He blew out the oil light and prepared to undress for bed when Kaifah's father appeared in the doorway, a lamp in his hand. He set it on a small table and settled himself on a bench by the wall. "The day has been fine," he began. "I hope you are enjoying your visit."

Hu assured him that he was.

"Of course one expects fine weather in dry season," he went on. "Up in your village in Laos do you plant rice as we do?"

"Well, yes, but not exactly. You see, we——"

"Yes, of course, each race has its own differences. I notice you speak Lao most of the time. Because we are quite close to Laos here, we speak Lao also. That's fortunate for you." He stopped to chuckle.

Hu began to say that he had known Lao much longer than Thai and that he was glad the two languages were similar, but the father interrupted again. "About my daughter, Kaifah," he said. "Have you come with her only as a visitor, or do you intend to ask for her in marriage? You see, our customs are no doubt different from yours, and if you intend . . ."

The older man rambled on, but Hu heard only the one blunt question. He found himself in a quandary of fear and uncertainty. "If I say I want to marry her," he thought, "Kaifah's father may well tell me the hopelessness of my dream, and that would be the end of everything. But if I stall for time and say I have come only for a visit, he may accuse me of destroying his daughter's reputation."

Suddenly he was aware of a silence. Kaifah's father had stopped talking and evidently expected him to say something. Hu decided the truth would be safest.

"Well, sir," he responded, taking a deep breath, "I came because I want to marry Kaifah."

"Very well," said the father, not at all surprised, "this is not for me to decide. We cannot stop our children, for it is, after all, their choice. I wouldn't want Kaifah to do anything against her will. In the morning we shall ask her if she is willing to go with you to your village."

By now Hu felt almost faint with excitement and fear. The father talked as though the idea were not at all out of the question. But still Hu feared that he might yet persuade Kaifah into refusing him.

Hu had been staring unseeing at the wall, but glancing at the older man, he saw that he was smiling kindly. "I have heard you are a good man, Ai Hu, but I still must call my older brother and talk to him. We will see him in the morning."

True to his word, the next morning the father brought the uncle in and introduced Hu to him. "We must ask the girl if she is willing," the uncle announced. They called Kaifah in and formally questioned her. "This man wants to marry you. He lives far away in Laos. Are you willing to go and live with him?"

Strangely enough, under the circumstances, Kaifah didn't seem nearly so shy as Hu remembered her in Bangkok. His heart sang at her reply: "I'll be happy to go with him," she said. "His village in Laos is not so far. I've been to Phuket, which is much farther. I'm willing to go with him."

"Very well," the father responded. "We have heard your answer." Then turning to Hu, he explained, "Tomorrow we shall meet with my brothers and sisters in town."

The next day Hu and Kaifah went with her father into the village to meet with the uncles and aunts. Once again they asked the girl if she would go with Hu and live in Laos, and once again Kaifah answered, "I am willing."

Then the older uncle said, "If that is the case, we can't prevent her from going. Now we must decide on how much we should ask for the engagement and the dowry price."

Much commotion buzzed among the assembled relatives. Hu trembled and thrilled by turns. One moment he felt like a prisoner about to be judged and fined. The next, he looked at Kaifah's serene face, and thrilled at the thought that she might some day be his. Could it be possible that he would really marry a Thai girl?

Finally out of the murmur and clamor of voices, the father spoke. "We have decided, Ai Hu. You must present us an engagement gift of ten thousand baht. To the girl you must give a gold ring and one thousand baht. This is surety so that if you don't marry her, the ring and the one thousand baht will be hers. On the other hand, if she deceives you and runs away, we will return to you the ten thousand baht."

Hu's heart shrank at the steep price. "As for the ten thousand baht," he explained, "I am only a poor student from a mountain village in Laos and can't afford that much money."

The clamor of voices rose again as the family discussed his reply. Finally, another relative said, "If you can't afford ten thousand baht, maybe you can pay five thousand."

"No, I am a poor student. I tell you I don't have that amount."

At this point the father left the room mumbling in an angry undertone. The relatives continued the discussion. "It really isn't fair to ask him so much," one said. "We didn't require it of the men that married our daughters."

"That's right," agreed another. "Some had to pay only a thousand baht or even four or five hundred."

The older uncle spoke again. "Do you think you could pay twenty-five hundred baht?"

Hu began to despair. The sum of twenty-five hundred baht was more than a year's savings on his meager mission allowance. Though he had set aside other money, he had not expected the dowry to be so great. "It is even as I told you," he persisted. "I am only a poor student. I don't have that much."

Prasan came over to sit by him. "I think you'd better agree to five thousand baht," he said quietly. "The father did ask ten thousand, and I know my brother. He will insist on no less than half."

"I know," Hu sighed, "but I can only pay two thousand."

"That wouldn't be right," Prasan insisted. "He requested ten thousand; so half would be about correct."

For several minutes Hu thought. It was against both his custom and his nature to let someone else best him in a bargain. Besides, it was quite true that he did not have five thousand baht with him at the moment. He glanced across the room at Kaifah. She smiled uncertainly at him, then lowered her gaze. How could he bear to lose her? What was five thousand baht anyway?

"I will pay it"—he announced at last—"the five thousand baht, though I can't give it all now. But I will have it by the wedding."

So the relatives all agreed, and the father came in. "How much cash can you pay today?" he asked.

"I have only a thousand baht with me."

"Well, pay us a thousand baht now. Then when you return to Bangkok, you can send us the other thousand. That will mean you owe us three thousand at the time of the marriage."

Once again before the assembled relatives the father addressed Kaifah. "Are you willing to marry this man and return with him to his village in Laos?"

The girl spoke clearly. "I would like to go and visit Hu's family and see his village, and then I'll decide for sure if I'll marry him and go to live with him."

All present agreed on the terms, and the group broke up.

Almost a year passed before Kaifah could visit Nam Yawn. By then Hu had almost finished his ministerial training course and expected to graduate in March. As part of his classwork he received an assignment to hold evangelistic meetings in his village. He wrote to Kaifah, who was still at home in Ubon, inviting her to come with him to meet his parents. Before Kaifah could arrive, however, Hu got a telegram saying that his father was sick, and he immediately took a bus for the north. Before leaving, he sent a telegram to Kaifah asking her to meet him in Chiang Khong, the Thai border town on the Mekong just down the river from Nam Yawn.

When Hu arrived home, he found his father weak but beginning to recover. The old man's heart had given him trouble before, and Hu always wondered when some serious seizure might take his father's life. Each night Hu called the people together. They appreciated his talks, for they had had less spiritual guidance while he had been gone. Several days later, word came that Kaifah and Prasan would reach Chiang Khong the following day. Hu went to where his father sat on his doorstep in the morning sun. Yang Si's wife sat quietly beside him. "Kaifah and her uncle are coming tomorrow," the son announced. "You know, Kaifah is the Thai girl that I am betrothed to marry."

DEMON OF PADENG

"It is hard for me to believe it, my son. Will you marry a Thai? Are you not afraid that after she has seen our simple ways, she will refuse you?" And the old man sighed deeply as he gazed across the village to the trees on the far bank of the Nam Yawn.

Hu smiled in the bright sunlight. "I have told her much about Nam Yawn, Father, and she has long wanted to see the place and to meet you and my stepmother. I know she will like my village." He spoke with a confidence greater than he felt. Then remembering Kaifah herself, he was glad again. "She is beautiful and slender, Father, with small hands like a princess, yet she works like a buffalo. I tell you she is pure silver all through."

The mother rose, saying she would bring medicine for the old man. Turning before she entered the house, she added, "We shall see. If she is as you claim, you are indeed a fortunate man. Many times beauty is not all that it promises."

The next morning Hu left for Chiang Khong. He knew he would find Kaifah and her uncle at the pastor's house on the bank overlooking the Mekong. At midday he disembarked from the riverboat, bade the boatman wait, and climbed the steep path up to the small wooden house. Coming up to the porch stairs, he could see them. Prasan and the pastor were talking, and Kaifah stood with her back to him. "Ah, yes, here is the bridegroom," Prasan cried. "We have just arrived, so you are in good time."

Hu barely nodded at the men. His attention centered on Kaifah, who turned just then with a smile. He had forgotten how lovely she was. Taking her hands he said, "I am glad you have come." Then he turned to Prasan. "Did you have a good journey?"

"Oh, yes, yes, a fine trip. He sees us at last," Prasan chuckled, turning to the pastor. "For a moment there I was not sure he knew we existed. And how is your father, Ai Hu?"

"Father is getting stronger, so that means we will hold the last meeting tonight in the village church, and tomorrow I shall return with you and Kaifah to Bangkok. But let us not delay longer. I have told the boatman to wait. Come." Bidding the pastor good-bye, the three started back down the path to the river, where the long, low-roofed boat floated. As soon as they settled on the benches, the motor sputtered and they started on their way.

The day was cool and clear, while the river reflected the gold and green of the forested hills on each bank. In the shallows near the shore, water buffalo waded knee-deep in the golden water. Occasionally a native boat, propelled by a standing oarsman, skimmed by, slim as a mango leaf.

"I am glad you will be able to journey with us tomorrow," Kaifah said a little too primly.

Hu sensed her coolness. "I didn't want to go ahead without you," he explained. "I feared you might not come at all."

"I very nearly stayed," she replied softly, "but Prasan encouraged me, and when he said he would come—well, here I am." She smiled a little and added, "And how is your father doing? Better, you say?"

"Oh, yes, or I would not plan to leave tomorrow. You see, the Father in the sky has done wonders for the old man. Two years ago it is now—yes, two years—my father had a bad attack with his heart. Ahjon Hawn was still here then. He helped me take my father all the way to the big mission hospital in Bangkok. The doctors there examined him, and Dr. Nelson said, 'He is an old man, and his heart is weak. We can do no more for him here. Let him go home to his family and live out his days in peace. Perhaps he has six months to live. Not much longer.' So we took him home.

"He was very weak by that time, since he had eaten nothing for some days, and he gathered us together and gave us his last counsels. But still he did not die. Then I remembered the story in God's Book about the good king Hezekiah. Do you remember?"

"No, I don't know the Bible well," Kaifah admitted softly, "but I would like to know it better."

"You will learn," Hu said, patting her hand. "King Hezekiah was dying. When he prayed and asked for healing, God extended his life. And I thought, maybe if we ask Him, God will also lengthen my father's life. I gathered my brothers and the mother, and we all prayed.

"My father remained weak for seven days. The eighth morning he got up and dressed, then walked out to the cookhouse and asked the mother to make him some soup. We all thought it was his last request. He knew he would die, so he was asking for his favorite food. But after he ate the food, he still sat and watched the women work. The next day he did the same thing, and each day he grew stronger until he was quite normal again. I thank God for what He has done. Already two years have gone by."

"I am glad you came quickly to see him, Hu." And Kaifah gave him a repentant smile. "It was proper that you come."

The boat began turning into the Laotian shore. "This is dry season," Hu explained, "so the river is low. We must get out on this sandbank and cross to the main shore yonder. Nam Yawn is a little more than an hour's walk from here."

They followed the route Hu pointed out. Walking across the sand and up the path from the river, they wended their way between the bamboo houses of a scattered Meo refugee village and on through the big trees into the Nam Yawn valley. On the way they met the usual tribal groups. One mule caravan and a *mahout* with his work elephant passed them, but not one wheeled vehicle did they see the whole morning. Finally they descended a low hill. The trees opened in a clearing, and the first bamboo houses of Nam Yawn appeared.

The visitors went first to Hu's father and stepmother, who greeted them warmly. Then the family led them to the bamboo cookhouse with its packed earth floor and a table with low wicker stools. Relatives brought steamed rice, fish, and green vegetables. After the meal they had a tour of the village. Much excitement prevailed, especially among the women, some of whom had put on their best clothes—skirts bordered with bright-colored embroidery and black blouses edged with embroidered flowers in pink and red. They followed the visitors closely, and Kaifah turned and smiled, reaching out to take the hands they extended to her. She stooped to look more closely at the pattern stitched on one sleeve. "I have never seen such fine embroidery in all of Thailand," she said.

The women giggled and chattered together with an air that spoke approval. Suddenly Kaifah said, "Where are the waterwheels, Hu? You know, the ones for threshing rice?"

"Never fear. We are coming to them," Hu answered. He stopped and held up his hand. "Listen. Do you hear them—that screaming sound that never stops?"

"Yes, of course. I have wondered ever since I came what that squealing was. It is the mill, you say?"

By then they had come in sight of the river, and there beyond the shrubbery rotated a waterwheel. The axle, a long tree trunk extending from the wheel to the shore, turned against wooden stakes that held it in place close to the ground. The rubbing against the stakes made the never-ending creaking. The village had four waterwheels, each with its hammers forever rising and falling on the rice in hollowed-out wooden mortars.

"These machines show fine workmanship," Prasan commented. "There are not many villages with this kind of convenience."

"No," agreed Hu, "you would have to walk far into the mountains to see other wheels like them. There are no others around here. Travelers often admire them, and for all these things we thank our Father in the sky. No rice, no mills, no food. The people of our village feel truly blessed."

That evening Hu called the people together for his farewell meeting, and the next morning he gathered his things preparatory to leaving. The visitors bade farewell to the old father as he sat on his front step. Kaifah took his hand in parting, and the old man said, "My son, you have reported the truth. She is pure silver as you said." He spoke in Meo so the visitors did not understand, but Yang Si's wife nodded approvingly.

The young couple turned to leave, and Hu whispered, "My father and mother like you, Kaifah. They were pleased with your visit."

The party returned as they had come, walking out along the jungle trail and taking the boat down the river. "I like your village," Kaifah said. "The people are friendly and skillful. I think I would not be afraid or lonely living there."

"And I would be with you," Hu added, putting his hand on hers, and he might have said more if he hadn't glimpsed Prasan's mischievous smile at just that moment.

DEMON OF PADENG

School closing activities crowded the next few weeks in Bangkok. Hu and Kaifah decided that they would have their wedding in Bangkok right after graduation in March. But before then there was just one more important assignment—a last series of meetings he would help conduct in Ban Dochi, Prasan's own village, and the home of Kaifah as well. The meetings were especially important to Hu, for he had hoped at that time that Kaifah, who had not yet joined the church, would make a public declaration of her faith. More than once she had told him of her wish to be baptized, so he was not surprised to see her faithfully in her seat each evening listening to the story of Vatiu Yesu.

During the day Hu kept busy with his ministerial duties—studying, visiting people, teaching the Bible to those interested. He had little time to spend with Kaifah, so he looked forward to seeing her each evening. Then there would be time for a few words together or perhaps a quick smile or a touch. Their visits weren't long, but Hu lived for those moments at the end of the day.

The meetings drew to a close. One week remained. Kaifah had made her decision to be baptized the last Sabbath of the series, and then they planned to return to Bangkok for Hu's graduation and their wedding. It was Wednesday evening of the last week. The meeting had ended, and Hu stood at the door, greeting the people. The last one had left, and he looked around for Kaifah. When he spotted her, he rushed over to her with his usual welcoming smile, but she gave none in return. "I am tired tonight, Hu," she said. "My head aches and I must go home." And saying no more she walked away with some of her girl friends.

What had he done? Hu tried hard to understand. She was tired, of course. That was what she had said, but it was not like her to complain of weariness. Could it be that now, at the last hour, she had decided that Nam Yawn was too far, that she didn't want to lose herself in a small obscure village? All night his thoughts tortured him, and he tossed restlessly on his mat.

The next day he wanted to seek out Kaifah and talk to her, but with a baptism planned for the Sabbath he had many people to visit; so he and Prasan spent the day visiting the candidates. That evening he did not wait until the meeting ended, but went to find Kaifah before she entered the hall.

She came in, surrounded with laughing girl friends. "Good evening, Hu," she greeted, her voice sweet but very cool. The presence of her friends made conversation impossible, and worst of all, Kaifah did not seem inclined to talk. Crushed, Hu turned away, and all through the meeting from his seat on the platform he heard scarcely anything. When he could bring himself to look at the girl, she seemed a distant and lovely dream, becoming ever more inaccessible.

After the meeting, one of the Thai pastors, Ahjon Sunti, noticed Hu's downcast face and asked him what the trouble was.

"It's Kaifah, Ahjon. I don't know what to think. I'm afraid——" His voice broke and his eyes filled with tears as he turned away.

"Really now, Ai Hu. I shall certainly speak to that girl tomorrow."

Next morning Ahjon Sunti met Hu as he tidied up around the hall. "Well, Ai Hu," he said, "I believe your fears were well founded. I wouldn't print my wedding cards if I were you. She doesn't plan to marry you."

The pastor went on his way. Hu leaned his broom against the doorjamb and sank into a chair. It was Friday. In a little more than a week he had hoped to marry Kaifah, but now . . . The slow tears coursed down his cheeks. He should have known. Somehow he had always found it hard to believe he would ever marry a Thai girl from a good house with——

The sound of voices made him jump up quickly. Brushing away his tears with the back of his hand, he seized the broom and began to sweep the floor furiously. A quick laugh rang outside, and Prasan burst in. "Oh, good morning, Ai Hu. You must be happy this morning. Only think, you will graduate in a few days and soon after— that's right, you have never told me. Exactly what day *is* the wedding?" Then he saw Hu's stricken face. "Why, what is wrong with you?"

"Prasan, the wedding is off. Kaifah has changed her mind." And he went on to explain what the pastor had told him.

DEMON OF PADENG

"Nonsense," blustered Prasan. "I have heard nothing of this. I shall certainly see about it." And before Hu could say anything the girl's uncle left.

Hu continued his chores, trembling between hope and fear at what Prasan might do. He worked in a kind of frenzy. Never had the little hall had such a cleaning.

Not until afternoon did Prasan appear again, whistling a merry tune. "Take heart, my good fellow," he said. "It is even as I suspected. Women! Sit down."

Hu sat down weakly and waited for his friend to explain. "I went to see my brother, and I asked him what the problem was about his daughter's changing her mind. He was amazed, knew nothing about it, and let me tell you he was angry. He called the girl in from the cookhouse and thundered, 'What is this we hear? What is this talk about changing your mind?' I have never heard him speak to her with such an angry tone. She is his favorite child. Kaifah began to cry."

"Oh, I hope he was not too severe with her."

"Not at all. The girl needed a shaking. She explained a great deal, but what the whole sum adds up to is she felt neglected and feared you didn't love her; so she was testing you."

"Didn't love her?" Hu gasped, and could find no more to say.

Prasan continued. "When the tears ended, she assured us that she still cares about you and wants to go through with the wedding. The father is having wedding cards printed this afternoon, and she is getting her dress ready. She reminded us that since she would be married in Bangkok in a Christian church, she intends to have a completely Christian wedding with a white dress and a veil like a cloud—those were her words. So have no fear, my good fellow. You will not escape. I suppose you will have the three thousand baht by next Sunday?"

"Oh, the money. There is no question about the money." Hu drew a long shuddering sigh and then smiled. "Now that I know there will be a bride," he added.

Chapter 7

DANGER IN THE WIND

Hu pushed his way through the last of the undergrowth and stepped out on a clear, rocky area. He had climbed as far as he could, and the great rock that was Padeng still towered above him so high that he felt it could topple over on him. Had any other Meo who yet lived ever dared to come where he stood? He doubted it. Terrible power was wielded by the spirit of that rock. It had struck people deaf, blind, or sick with fever. Crops under its face had refused to grow. Yet, here he was, Hu Sae Yang, and he felt no fear. Though he knew the spirits existed and did not for a moment doubt their malevolent power, he also realized that the Father who lived in the sky was greater than all. He had seen it proved again and again. Looking beyond the peak to the clear heaven, he said, "Thank You, good Father of the sky. Thank You for Your protection of me, a poor mountain boy, who, because of You, stands here in this place without feeling afraid."

The afternoon sun struck the peak, and Hu searched its face for some clue as to why people called it *pa deng*, "red cliff," but he spotted nothing. No doubt the reason was lost in history, but he could spend no more time musing about it. The afternoon was passing, and he knew he must start home. He had told his father he would hunt for his lost goats, and so far the search had yielded nothing. But he was in good humor, for his main purpose in taking the hike had been to climb to Padeng. It had been his secret plan for a long time, and now he had done it.

With a last look at the rugged peak, he turned back into the jungle on his way down to the village. Since there was no path, he simply continued in the southerly direction which led back to his valley. He passed through thick jungle and into a dark ravine before he finally climbed the last hill that bordered the Nam Yawn valley.

Reaching the crest of the hill, he found the trees thinning enough so that by climbing on a boulder he had a good view of his valley. He stopped to pick out familiar objects. The sun gleamed on the corrugated iron roof of the church and the little school building, and to the right of them, his own house. It had been a proud day for Nam Yawn when the villagers had constructed the church and school of lumber and iron. They had hired some Thais to saw the logs, for the Meo knew nothing of using carpenters' tools. Now they had permanent buildings that they would not have to replace every two or three years like the old bamboo houses.

Hu also felt proud of the fine house he had built for Kaifah. She told him she liked it as well as any in Ban Dochi, her own village. It stood on posts high off the ground, and though the walls consisted of woven bamboo, he had built the floors of sawn lumber polished smooth and had erected a roof of strong corrugated iron. Hu also had gotten Kaifah a foot treadle sewing machine, as well as a concrete stove for their cookhouse, much like the one he had seen at his father-in-law's home. They had no tiled bath place, but Kaifah said she enjoyed bathing in the river. Down the path behind the house was a sealed pit latrine, a wonder of sanitation for a Meo village. The other village people also had latrines. That, along with the fact that the village contained no pigs, made it a much cleaner place than most tribal settlements, and passing travelers marveled at it continually.

From his vantage point Hu could see the tangerine orchard to the right of the village and near it the hazy green of the mulberry trees the mission had sent them to plant. When the trees grew big enough, the villagers hoped to begin raising silkworms so they would have raw silk to sell to the Thais, who wove it into cloth. That would be a few years in the future yet, but the tangerine orchard was already bearing. It was the first season the trees had done well, and the whole village feasted on the fruit.

He was too far away to see the movement of people in the

village, but he imagined that Kaifah might be returning from the orchard about now. Probably their little boy would be with her. Hu had never thought he could love an adopted child so much. After two years of marriage, when no baby had come, Hu had talked to Ahjon Wick, who had counseled him to adopt a child if Kaifah was willing. They had decided to adopt a baby boy on one of their visits back to Thailand. The child was two years old now, bright and healthy, and Kaifah was happy with an infant to care for.

The young Meo husband had never lost his sense of good fortune whenever he thought of Kaifah. She had learned the Meo language quickly and had taught the other women what she knew of sewing, cooking, and sanitation. Some months after Kaifah had first arrived in Nam Yawn, Ahjon Pangan and his wife, Fel, had visited them. Fel had taught the women to sew clothes for their children. Remembering what Ahjon Pangan had said before he left, Hu smiled. "Your wife has done very well, Ai Hu. I had some misgivings when I thought of a Thai girl moving to this isolated place. Some of them are rather spoiled, but she is not. She has proved herself a real treasure."

Perhaps it was Kaifah herself who had summed things up best. "You are Meo and I am Thai," she had said one day. "But really it is unimportant, because we are Christians." Yes, that was the secret: the strong love of the Father in the sky spread all around them like sunlight.

His eye fell on the house of Cheng Sae Mua. Now there was another example of God's blessing. Cheng's wife had had treatment for malaria shortly after the birth of her baby in Chiang Khong. Her fever went down, and she returned home to Nam Yawn. But in a few weeks the fever came back again. She went to Houei Sai to get medicine, but it didn't help her. Her parents, who lived in a village in Thailand, got permission for her to go to the hospital in Chiang Rai for treatment, where she stayed a week receiving medicine and blood transfusions for her anemic condition. For a time she seemed to get well, and she went back to Nam Yawn. But again the fever returned, only much worse. Once more she traveled to Chiang Rai and seemed to get well. When the fever returned the next time, it was worse than ever. She could not rise from her bed, had frequent lapses into unconsciousness, and was too weak to endure the long trip on the bus back to Chiang Rai, even if the doctors could cure her. So far they hadn't. Hu remembered the hopeless frustration of her young husband. "There is nothing we can do, Hu. She sleeps and does not waken, and I fear she will die."

"There *is* something we can do," Hu replied. "In His Book, the Father tells us by James that we should call the elders to anoint the sick with oil and pray for healing. That is what we can do." And they did. The sick girl remained about the same for four days.

Then she began to improve, becoming progressively stronger, and after some weeks, when she seemed quite normal again, her husband took her to Chiang Rai for an examination. The physician tested and observed her. Finally the doctor said, "You have no malaria and are well." Once more she returned to Nam Yawn. That had been two months before, and she was still healthy.

Then there was Ai Chew Yee and his wife. Three days after the birth of their boy, the mother noticed sores behind his ears and in his groin, and the baby could not move his legs. On the fourth day Hu gathered the elders to pray for the child, requesting God to heal him if it was His will. They saw no immediate change, but the mother tried to follow the simple sanitary care Hu taught her. After a month the sores cleared up and the baby began to move its toes. The child was nine months old now, strong and normal. The last time Hu had seen him, he had been learning to walk.

And of course there was his father, still with them six years after the doctor had given him six months to live. No doubt existed in Hu's mind that a great and loving Person had His hand over Nam Yawn and its people.

Suddenly a faint cry—the bleating of goats—startled him out of his reverie. Walking toward some large boulders on his right from where he heard the cry, Hu began calling. There they came, the three lost ones—a black male and two black and white females. He herded them toward the trail that led from the clearing to the valley. As he started down the path, keeping the goats ahead of him, he noticed four men also walking along the trail ahead of him.

DEMON OF PADENG

By their olive-green clothes he recognized them as soldiers. They turned once and glanced back at him but did not wait for him or speak to him. A little farther down the hill, the trail disappeared into the trees, and when Hu reached that point the soldiers had vanished. They were insurgents, he had no doubt, for it was common knowledge among the tribespeople in the area that the guerrillas had an encampment about an hour's hike from Nam Yawn.

Their appearance raised a dark train of thought in his mind. Only yesterday he had received a letter from Bangkok. Ahjon Pangan had asked if it would be safe for him to come to Nam Yawn, bringing some Americans who wanted to see the village. Usually Hu and his people were happy for Christian visitors from the outside world, and a visit from an ordained pastor was often necessary. Even now people waited for baptism in Nam Yawn and in the neighboring village of Pak Ngao. But now Hu felt uneasy.

Lately, passing travelers had brought rumors about new army movements. Unrest was spreading among the Meo mercenaries hired by the Americans to fight the insurgents. The money left with the Lao government to pay the soldiers was not getting to them. The soldiers felt sure it was going into the pockets of corrupt generals at headquarters, and they threatened to join the opposition. The people whispered that they planned on taking Houei Sai, the nearby provincial capital. If that happened, the insurgents would control the Nam Yawn area, and then who knew what might happen? What should he tell the pastor? He must write a letter and send it to be mailed in Chiang Khong tomorrow, but he wondered what he should say.

Then he thought of Pak Ngao. Four people awaited baptism in that village just a few kilometers away. Somehow Hu felt that the baptism must take place. God had done great things there, and surely He would want the baptism to go on. Pak Ngao was another refugee settlement that had been established by the people of Nam Yu, an inland Meo village captured by the insurgents. Some three hundred people had fled and built their bamboo houses on both sides of a long dusty road that followed the course of a small river.

Ahjon Hawn had brought the knowledge of God to the people while they were still in Nam Yu, and there seventeen families had asked him to perform the zia da for them. They had cut off all connection with the spirits and committed their lives to the protection of the Creator-God. The invasion threat had forced the pastor to leave before he could instruct the people further or baptize them. Finally the people, too, had had to flee before the invaders. When the villagers finally settled on their new site, in the midst of the long row of houses stood the seventeen homes of those who had "burned the spirits."

A few months after the people settled there, sickness spread among them. The mountain people, not used to life in the lowlands, struggled with an epidemic of dysentery and malaria. The progress of the illness seemed orderly. People in the houses at one end of the street became sick, then those in the next house and the one beyond that. People began to die. More than one spirit doctor was continually busy, and the throb of death drums filled the air from dawn till dark. But amid all the sorrow, confusion, and suffering, those who still lived began to realize something. A strange phenomenon took place. Hu later heard of it from many witnesses.

People passing in the road would say to one another, "Have you seen? Have you heard? There is no illness at the house of See Sae Kao."

"What of that? There are others too who are not yet sick. I for one."

"Yes, but your daughter died. No one has yet sickened in the house of See Sae Kao. But that is not all. The families of Phoo, of Shong Sat, of Dah Shua—you know. Those seventeen houses are all untouched. None are sick."

"Ah, yes, we shall see. The plague is not over yet."

"Very well, we shall wait. But I think it is even as See told me. They are no longer under the spirits. They worship the Creator-Father and His Son, Vatiu Yesu. And See says they are stronger than Da-nyu-va. I begin to believe he is right."

By the time the epidemic ended, those who survived in Pak Ngao had to admit that the God of the seventeen Christian families had done great things. In the whole village more than a hundred people had died, but not one of the seventeen had perished. None of them had even been sick.

After the plague many people, fearful of some spirit curse, had left to settle elsewhere. Most of the Christian families had moved either to Nam Yawn or to villages in Thailand where other Christians lived. The village remained, however, and now two young men and the wife of a spirit worshiper along with her daughter waited for baptism.

"After what God has done there," Hu thought, "we must not delay baptism. I will tell Ahjon Pangan and the visitors to come. God will care for them and for us." The decision made, his mind felt easier. He emerged from the jungle, the goats running before him as he skirted the edge of the village.

Just then he looked up to see three travelers approaching. Hu recognized them as Meo tribesmen walking north. They greeted him and then stopped as if they wanted to speak to him. "My name is Choo Sae Kan," the oldest man said. "These are my sons. We live in the next village north and often pass by here. I know this is a Christian village, and we have often wondered which mission you belong to. They must pay you well, for you have fine strong buildings and water mills and orchards."

Hu understood what the man meant, for some of the other missions did subsidize their believers because the people had no opium crops for cash. With a laugh he replied, "No, indeed. It is quite the other way. We are the ones who pay."

"You pay?" the men responded in surprise.

"Yes, we pay one tenth of all we gather from our crops of rice. It is not the mission that commands us. It is the Father in the sky. In His Book of Instruction He has told us to bring a tenth and put it in His storehouse. When the people thresh their rice, they bring every tenth basket and pour it into a large storage bin under my house. That rice we take to town and sell, and we send the money to the mission, where they use it to tell more people about the great Father."

"Why," said one of the younger travelers, "I don't see how you can afford to pay that much out. I could not."

"If you knew the Father," Hu answered reverently, "you would be glad to. You see, He covers us with His hand. No spirits curse us; so we sacrifice no animals. He heals our sickness and makes our fields grow. We are greatly blessed. He promises to bless those who pay Him His tenth, and He keeps His word."

Suddenly the sound of a happy voice came to their ears. Along the path a little girl came walking, singing with all her heart.

> "Beautiful Yesu, Maker of all things,
> Son of God and Son of man,
> You are my joy.
> You are my song."

The little girl walked past them, looking neither to right nor left, while her clear, sweet voice piped on until she turned a corner, and it faded in the distance.

The old man watched her intently. "She is blind, the little one?"

"Yes," Hu said. "The evil spirits closed her eyes before her parents had the wisdom to follow the great Father."

"Why does she sing, being blind?"

"You heard her words. She loves Vatiu Yesu. The instructions tell us that Vatiu Yesu is coming to the earth again. And when He does He will give His children new bodies. That little one will have eyes that see again."

"If I could only know there *is* such a Father," the old man said.

Silence lingered a moment as the men thought about what they had heard. Suddenly one of the young men looked up. The others followed his gaze. A half dozen olive-clad men walked down the road away from the village. They moved on and soon disappeared in the late afternoon light.

"I fear we will have trouble soon," the old one commented.

"There is danger in the wind," his son answered.

"Yes," Hu added, "there is danger, but Yesu has said, 'In the world you will have great trouble, but be glad, for I have overcome the world.' "

DEMON OF PADENG

Chapter 8

PHUA SAE LEE AND THE TIGER SPIRIT

"I remember you. You are Hu Sae Yang." The man's voice was tense, his face drawn with pain. "If you can do something—if you know of a god who is good, I want to know. The spirits are killing me."

Hu looked at the patient in the hospital bed. He could see the resemblance now. Sixteen years before he had met him in Nam Phet, a village some 40 kilometers from Nam Yawn. At that time Hu had spent two weeks preaching there. The man, Phua Sae Lee, had listened, but he had turned away. Young then, liking native liquor and his laughing friends, Phua had been much too proud to take seriously a strange message from a sixteen-year-old boy. Hu had almost forgotten him until yesterday afternoon when he had visited a Christian family in a village across the river. The wife of the family had begged him to visit her brother Phua, who was seriously sick in the hospital in Houei Sai.

The pleading voice broke into his thoughts. "Do you know of a god who is good? Maybe your god will listen if you ask him to help." At that point the man threw aside the sheet that covered him. Hu could see that one of his legs had swollen to twice its natural size, and a wad of cotton covered most of a large ulcer on the foot.

"It is not my leg only," the sick man continued. "Since this morning I have had terrible dysentery. Every few minutes I have to leave my bed. I am passing blood, and I fear I will die." Phua sighed, his eyes shadowed with fear, beads of sweat gathering on his forehead.

"It is the tiger spirit," he said, his voice hushed. "She has tormented me for years. You will find it hard to believe, perhaps, but yesterday morning I was almost well. My leg was its normal size. I had no diarrhea. And my wife had come, intending to stay until I left for home." He indicated a young woman with a sad face and haunted eyes who sat so quietly in the corner that Hu had scarcely noticed her.

The man continued his story. "We knew she would need rice while she was here. The hospital feeds patients but not visitors; so we sent to our village for rice, and a neighbor brought it yesterday afternoon. Almost as soon as he left, my leg swelled up again, and the small wound opened up into the big sore you see now. Amazed, the doctors could not account for it. Then all through the night the windows rattled, and an unseen hand pounded the wall there over my head. It is my tormenting spirit. Unseen, she came with the man who brought the rice, and I fear she will kill me. Is there no help for me, Ahjon?"

"Yes," Hu answered quietly, "there is. The great God of the sky, the Creator, has power over the evil spirits. I will ask Him to help you." Standing by the bed, Hu took the man's hand and asked the Lord to drive away the evil spirits, to heal Phua, and to give peace to him and his family.

Phua drew a long sigh. "Somehow, I feel better already," he said. "Oh, you cannot imagine all I have suffered. For some reason I am under a great curse."

Sensing that the man had a story to tell, Hu sat down again and waited.

"I was not always as you see me," Phua began. "You remember me in happier days. Years ago when you told me of the Father in the sky, I was young and strong and saw no reason to change my religion. I had no need then I thought. Soon after that I married the first time, and my wife and I lived contentedly for a time. We had two children, and they seemed healthy enough. But then my wife's mother died, and soon after, her father. We had a fine funeral for each death and made great sacrifices, but for some reason the spirits of both the father and the mother could not find rest. Almost every night they came back to torment my wife. In the middle of the night I would hear her scream and gasp out, 'They hold my throat. I cannot breathe.' The next night they might return and demand chicken to eat.

"We would fall asleep exhausted and waken at dawn. Before it was fully light my wife would catch a chicken, kill and feather it, cut it up, and cook it. Then she would go out in the yard and set out the meat on a high post behind the house so no animals could reach it. And as we have been taught, she did not stay to watch but quickly turned her back on it and returned to the house. A few minutes later as we peered through the cracks in the bamboo wall we could see the meat had vanished. The neighbors, you say? Oh, no, Ahjon, not in our village. The whole village fears the spirits so much that they will not even come into my house. By now the terror is so great that no tu-ua-neng will visit our house anymore. But I run ahead of my story.

"My first wife, poor creature, suffered torments night after night. She offered the chicken in the morning, and always it vanished from the post. Then the spirits grew bolder. One evening when she returned from working in the field, our oldest boy, who was almost six years old then, ran out of the house full of excitement. 'Grandmother was here today,' he cried. 'She sat on a stool by the fire and held her hands out to sister and me. Then she talked with us, and just before she left, Grandfather stood over there in the corner for a little while.' More than once the children reported their visits to us.

"Then my wife had a third child, a boy, and after that, the spirit sickness began to torment her. Every small thing became great. If she woke with a little headache, soon the pain became so severe that she would lie moaning on her bed, helpless. Or if she scratched her finger on a splinter while splitting wood, her arm would swell enormously, and she could do no work at all. We called the tu-ua-neng, and he would bargain with the spirits. After we would offer a chicken as the spirits asked, the ailment would usually go away.

"But sometimes the sickness didn't leave. One day a small fever turned into a great sickness. We called the spirit doctor and sacrificed chickens. No relief. Again we called him and offered a pig, but she only became worse. Once more we summoned the spirit man, but he refused to come. 'It is of no use,' he said. 'The spirits are determined to have her.' He was right. Two days later she died.

"I was sad and much afraid. Besides, I had three little children—the youngest only five months old—with no mother. The baby cried all the time, for I had no milk to give him. The neighbors feared to help us. Because they believed the spirits were angry and had put a curse on my house, they would not come near us.

"One day as I walked to the rice field to harvest my grain, I saw my wife on the path ahead of me. She was no farther away than that palm tree out there—so close that I could see her face and the embroidery pattern on her skirt. There was no mistake, but as I ran to meet her, she vanished from my eyes.

"I felt all the more lonely after that, but somehow I managed to cut down the grain and gather it up. One day, soon after, I took the three children with me and went back to my rice field to pound out the grain. I stood by my stack of rice and looked about the field. All my neighbors had finished their work long before, and here I was with so much threshing to do and no one to care for the children. My oldest boy clung to my jacket, and I carried my girl on one arm and the baby on the other, and both were wailing. If only my wife were here, I thought. She could care for them while I thresh the rice. Then I remembered seeing her on the path a few days before. Maybe she wasn't really dead. Perhaps her spirit could help me. I called her then, three times. 'Inchow, wherever you are, come help me. Inchow! Inchow!'

"Suddenly, across the field I heard the sound of feet striking the earth, but not like a person walking. It was the sound of a cow running. The grass and weeds parted under the weight of heavy hooves, but I could not see the thing that made it. When something passed close by, I grew cold with fear. Putting down the children, who had frozen into silence, I grabbed the gun I always carry. I fired in the direction the thing had gone, but nothing happened. My heart pounded so hard I could hardly breathe. Well, I can tell you I never called my wife again.

"The days dragged on miserably. Somehow I managed to thresh

the rice. The baby cried most of the time. I tried to feed him rice, or sometimes bananas or cooked yam, but none of it was good food for a baby. One morning I awoke, and the baby was quiet. Thinking he was sleeping, I touched him, only to find him cold as stone. I sat down and wept then and thought how the spirits had taken my wife and now my son, and I wondered when they would come after me.

"Time went by and somehow the other children and I managed to survive for two more years. Then I met Kua, here." Phua indicated his young wife, who smiled shyly and looked away. "Her husband had left her with a little baby to care for, and she needed a protector. I surely needed help, too, so she became my second wife.

"But even now I am not at peace. I suffer from the spirit sickness like my first wife did. It simply means that for me every little hurt turns into a great sickness. A small pain becomes so bad I fall in a faint and have to have someone put me to bed. A few months ago I started out to another village with my friends, and while I walked, a pain attacked my head. It became so severe that I fell down in a faint. My friends had to carry me home."

"How do you know all this is from the spirits?" Hu asked.

"When I call the tu-ua-neng, he tells me to offer a sacrifice, and as soon as we present the chicken, I am well."

"Always?"

"Well, no, not when the spirits are angry. Not this time, as you can see."

"Now that you have a wife again, are things not better?"

"Things would be well with us, I think, if the spirits would but leave us alone." The man sighed deeply as he passed his hand across his eyes.

The young wife bit her lip and lowered her gaze as if to hide her tears.

"Almost every night they torment me. When I lie down on my bed and my new wife joins me on the mat, the spirit of my first wife comes on the other side of me. She puts her cold hands on my throat and squeezes my neck and tries to strangle me. I am so frightened that I cannot move at first. I lie cold with fear. When I can move again, I grab my gun—I always keep it by my bed along with two large knives—and try to shoot the dim shape when it appears, but it does no good. The neighbors could tell you about the gunshots in the middle of the night. They always ask me about them. But no one can help me.

"The last time I called for the tu-ua-neng, he refused to come. I went to the two others in the village. They wouldn't aid me either. 'This spirit is powerful and very fierce,' they tell me. 'Your wife is a tiger, and no one can control tiger spirits. We do not dare visit your house anymore, for then she might start to bother us.' "

The young wife was crying softly, wiping her tears on the faded embroidery of her skirt. "He thinks of nothing but his spirit wife," she sobbed.

"Yes," Phua went on, "we quarrel much about this. When I get sick, she says it is because I draw the spirit to me. Of course when I am sick, Kua also has more work to do. But I tell her always that I love her more than the terrible tiger spirit, and I do."

The man paused a moment and glanced about uneasily. His wife stared vacantly into space, tears still wet on her cheeks. Hu thought he had never seen two more despairing souls. "What injury brought you your present sickness?" Hu asked at last.

"Oh, it was like all the rest, almost nothing at first—only a small insect bite on my foot. But like the other times, the small became great. My leg swelled, and the little spot became a great open sore. I offered many chickens, but it did no good. Finally they brought me here, and the doctors treated me. After a few days the swelling went down, and the sore healed. I was much better by the time my wife arrived. Then, even as I told you before, the tiger spirit came yesterday with the man who brought the rice. As soon as he left, my leg swelled, the sore burst open, the windows rattled, and something pounded the wall."

Hu stood up. "The hour grows late, Phua. It will soon be night; so I must go. I can tell you only that the great Creator, the One I prayed to a few minutes ago concerning you, is your hope. He is stronger than the spirits. He cares about you and loves you, but He cannot save you unless you let Him. If you ask Him to be your protector, you will have nothing to fear."

DEMON OF PADENG

Phua nodded. "Please, Ahjon, come to Nam Phet sometimes. I want to hear more."

Almost two weeks passed before Hu heard anything more of Phua. Then one day Yee returned from the village of outer Nam Yawn with the news that he had met a man sent by Phua who said, "Tell Hu to come quickly. I am much worse, and likely I'll die."

The next morning Hu started the long journey on the rough, steep mountain trail. Drizzling rain fell most of the day. By late afternoon he was wet through and bone weary as he tried to keep his footing on the slippery clay of the high trail. When he had walked nine hours, he began to wonder if he had lost his way. Early darkness was closing in under the gray sky when he finally came upon the village. But enough light still lingered so he could see that Nam Phet was a large settlement with a big wooden Christian church at its center. The first man he met knew where Phua lived, and Hu soon stood in front of a large bamboo house. Barking dogs heralded his arrival, and two half-grown children peered from the door, then ran in shouting, "He's here, Father. He's come."

Hu entered then and saw by the light of the cook fire that Phua lay stretched out on his platform bed, his leg wrapped in rags.

"Oh, my friend, I am so glad to see you. I was sure I would die before you got here. No one wanted to go and get you. Finally I had to pay a man. You see, the whole village is in terror of the spirit."

Damp, hungry, and aching with exhaustion, Hu sank down gratefully on the wicker stool Kua had set by the fire for him. "I am glad to be here at last. I took the wrong road back there, so my journey was longer than necessary, and I am very tired."

"I know," Phua sympathized, "and I thank you for coming, but you must not sleep until we have had zia da. I insist that you perform the ritual without delay."

"No, no," said Hu, his voice emphatic. "You don't understand. It is not some magic we do, something we play at. The ritual has no strength in itself. The power comes from knowing the Father and His Son, Yesu." Hu moved closer to the sick man, his weariness forgotten. "We conduct no haggling, coaxing ceremony like the witch doctor does. You, my friend, must make a decision—you must choose to break completely with the spirits."

"And that is exactly what I want," Phua answered. "I am weary of all the torment. Since the spirits will kill me soon anyway, I have nothing to lose." The sick man propped himself up, leaning his arm on a chunk of firewood. "My first wife used to beg me to call in the Christian leader here in the village and have zia da. But I never would, because I noticed that the Christians around here would have zia da performed, then if things looked bad or they got sick and the American medicine didn't cure them right away, they went back to the tu-ua-neng. I didn't see that their Christianity had much to offer, so I am glad to hear you talking about a complete break with the spirits.

"Now," Phua continued, "let me tell you why we must have zia da tonight. After you prayed for me at the hospital, I began to get well. The diarrhea stopped and the swelling went down in my leg. In a few days only a tiny sore remained. The doctor told Kua how to bandage it and sent me home with some medicine. But as you see, it is rainy season. The rain and mud made my foot bad again. It swelled up, and the sore became worse than ever."

Hu got up from his stool and went over to examine the foot more closely. He shook his head at the exposed tendons.

Phua grimaced with pain and went on with his story. "Five nights ago Kua and I were preparing for bed when we heard the sound of a large animal walking around the house. It sounded like a cow, but we knew all the village cattle were securely penned on the other side of the village. Yet we could hear thudding hooves and heavy breathing and also the noise of something heavy dragging on the ground. We peered out between the cracks but saw nothing. The tramping went on for some time while I lay here sick and helpless, and my wife and children crouched near the fire not daring even to whisper. Finally the thing went away, and we fell on our mats exhausted. But I didn't sleep. My leg pained me greatly, and I was frightened.

"Next morning my wife and children ran out in the yard to investigate. They should have found many tracks in the mud, but there was not a one. Then I heard one of the children shouting, followed by a scrambling sound on the roof. My wife came running inside. She screamed something about the dog and how they had seen it walking on the roof. 'It is the spirit sign of death,' she cried. 'Oh, Phua, you will die.' And she began to weep.

"When she said that, I grew cold with fear and began to tremble. It seemed that my doom was certain. Any Meo knows that sign. If he sees a large animal on his roof, it is such an unnatural thing that it means death. Because I knew all the spirit men had given me up long before, I didn't even summon them. I had no hope but you and your God, Ahjon. Three days ago I sent word to you. Three days I have lain here trembling between life and death. Do you wonder that I say we must have zia da tonight?"

Hu smiled. "Fear no more, my brother. Your deliverance has come."

"But you can eat a little," Kua interrupted. She pushed a plate of rice and a spoon into his hands, and Hu, sitting by the fire, ate hurriedly.

When he had finished, Hu opened his bundle. "I want to tell you now about Vatiu Yesu and how He has conquered not only the spirits but all evil." From his bundle he produced a large picture roll which he hung on a nail on the wall and set a lighted lantern near it. The picture showed a white-robed man with a noble face commanding a strange, proud-faced being with shadowy wings.

"This picture represents Vatiu Yesu, the great Creator. He and His Father and the Holy Spirit are the Ones we call God. Together they made the world and man and even the spirits. This is why Yesu is stronger than they are. All the spirits were good at first, but they rebelled against the will of the good God, and He had to cast them out of the heaven where God dwells.

"It is not the spirits of your dead who afflict you. God's Book says the dead are asleep and know nothing. It is these rebellious spirits who attack you. Having the power to take any form they wish, they have as their main purpose to deceive men. They are stronger than we are because they are more than physical. Guns and knives cannot touch them, but Vatiu Yesu is all-powerful. The evil spirits tremble at His name because He is good. Keep Him and His goodness in your mind. There is no evil at all in Him. When He promises something, He honors His word. To His children He says, 'Fear not. I am with you always.' When we ask Him to, He gives us His goodness and we are then accounted perfect in God's eyes. Then He turns our hearts around and helps us do good instead of evil."

"But why should He do this?" Phua asked. "Do we give nothing in return? No sacrifice? No chickens or pigs or bullocks? Does not your God require blood?"

"It is true," Hu said. "We ought to bring a sacrifice, but we are not good, and we have nothing suitable for a good God. Really, we deserve to die. But God loves us. That is why long ago Yesu Himself came to earth and became a man. These same evil spirits caused rebellious men to kill Him. They fastened Him to a cross of wood they made. Yes, that's right, with nails they did it. They drove them through His hands and feet."

Hu turned the pages of his roll until he found a picture illustrating his words. "This was God's sacrifice. He made it because we couldn't. He did it because He loves us. We do not have to kill animals. The blood of Vatiu Yesu is enough for all people always."

"I am so glad," Kua said, her eyes bright with tears. "I am so happy that the One who is strongest is also the One who is good." She shook her head ruefully. "Only think. All these years we have lived in dread for nothing."

"Well, my friends, you need fear no more," Hu smiled. "Now we must burn every object you used to worship the evil powers." He rose from his stool and strode across the room. From the north wall he tore down the spirit shelf and the spirit paper. Smeared on the paper was chicken's and pig's blood along with feathers and bristles. He threw them on the kitchen fire.

"And now the spirit of the old pig," he said.

Kua pointed up to the central beam of the house. Hu laughed and called over the oldest child, a boy of eight or nine. "Would you like to help us, little son?" And picking him up, he lifted the youth as high as he could. "Here, untie the neck bone of the old pig. Can you reach it, my boy?"

DEMON OF PADENG

"The knot is tight. I can't untie it," the child said, struggling hard.

"Give him a knife, Kua."

With the knife the child soon severed the cords and the small bone fell to the earth. Kua herself picked it up and tossed it on the fire.

"Now the spirit of the door."

"Over here," Phua pointed above his bed. "I hung it here, hoping it would heal me. Take it down and burn it quickly, for it has brought me nothing but evil."

By standing on a stool on the platform bed, Hu managed to reach the cloth bag suspended from a beam. He opened it and shook out a long-necked gourd—split in half to make a ladle—and nine cups fashioned from a stem of bamboo. The ladle Phua had used to pour pig broth into the cups as an offering whenever he had sacrifices made. Hu hurled the objects into the fire, and last of all their bag. The fire blazed brightly, and Hu sat on a stool near its warmth and light. "I will teach you a song now. Listen well. Then when the spirits come or whenever you are afraid, you can sing it."

> "Yesu is my good friend.
> He carries all my troubles.
> No one loves me as far as Yesu.
> He helps me escape from the spirits' power
> And holds me in His arms.
> No one can make me afraid."

The flames burned low. Silence filled the house. "And now we will pray," Hu said. "Bow your heads and fold your hands like this. Father who lives in the sky, we thank You that You have given us Yesu. Now I present to You Phua and Kua and their children. They want to be Your children, under Your protection. Help them to trust You. Help them to pray when the spirits come. We ask You in the name of Vatiu Yesu. Amen."

The fire had died to red coals, and only the sound of wind and rain came to their ears. Hu smiled. "This house is safe now."

"May the good Father make it so," Phua said fervently.

"And now, my friend," Hu laughed, "if you don't mind, I would like to sleep."

"Yes, yes, you shall indeed. Kua, bring mats to lay by the fire." Phua began sliding himself off his platform.

"No, no. Guest I may be, but I will not take your bed. You stay there off the ground so your foot will heal. The Father heals, but He expects us to follow the laws of health."

As Phua obeyed, Hu stretched out on the mat by the fire and fell asleep almost immediately.

The next morning Hu awoke as Kua lighted the fire for breakfast. She set her pot of rice on the iron rack over the flames and took down the wicker table from its place on the wall.

Phua sat up. "It is the first good sleep in many weeks," he said. He wriggled the toes of his sore foot. "My leg feels better."

"You will be well soon, Phua, now that you have put yourself under God's care," Hu said. "I will treat your leg with water before I leave."

After breakfast Hu told Kua to set a pot of water on the fire, and when the water boiled, he took from his pack an old woolen blanket cut into squares. He folded one of the squares in thirds, dipped it into the water, and wrung it out by twisting it. Then he wrapped the steaming cloth in a dry square and packed it around the sick man's leg. For twenty minutes he continued the treatment. Then after leaving medicine with the man and praying again with the family, Hu left on his long walk home.

Two weeks later Hu returned. Arriving before nightfall, he found Phua in his yard cutting wood.

"Oh, my friend," he greeted Hu. "I am glad you have come back. As you see, I am well."

"I am happy to see that. But really, it is what I expected."

"Yes, I am having health and peace for the first time in years." Phua leaned his ax against a log and waved his arm toward the neighboring houses. "You know, this whole village is watching me and my family. They all know what I have suffered and how the spirits have tormented me." Chuckling, he pointed his thumb over his shoulder. "The witch doctors"—he lowered his voice—"are especially watching this battle. They say, 'If this God can really keep away such a powerful spirit, we will also burn the spirits, but if the spirits take control again, we will never be Christians.' "

"I would guess the spirit has not returned."

"Well, it did come back last week." Phua grinned. "Kua and I were resting by the fire one evening when we heard heavy footsteps walking slowly back and forth on the roof. It sounded like a person, and finally it seemed as if he sat down over there on the corner of the roof. We were quite frightened. I walked softly over to the corner to get my gun.

"Kua said, 'No, Phua, don't do that. A gun does no good with spirits.'

"But I was so afraid I couldn't think. I said, 'I will teach that spirit a lesson.'

"Kua was wiser than I was that time. She said, 'No, Phua, they are stronger than we are. Don't you remember? Ahjon said we must pray to God. He will drive away the spirits.'

"Finally I realized what she was saying. I said, 'Oh, I forgot. I thought I was still worshiping the spirits. Let us ask God.'

"So we bowed our heads, and I prayed, 'Great God of the sky, we are weak, but You are strong. Please make the spirit go away.' And you know, Ahjon, we heard a sound as if someone or something was being struck down, and then the noise of feet running. All the dogs in the village set up a howling and a barking as they followed those feet into the jungle. The racket was terrible. The whole village heard the noise, but they feared to come and investigate. The next day I told them what had happened. The spirit has not returned."

"Praise God," Hu said. "This is God's power, not ours, and He is always willing to protect those who trust Him."

"Ahjon," Phua said, a smile lighting his face, "I want to be God's man. You see how even in this little while I am getting strong and fat. Ahjon, I know it is far—nine hours—for you to travel here, but will you come every two weeks to teach us? I want to know more so I can believe more."

"It is the work God has given me to do. Of course I will come."

Chapter 9

GOD IS NOT LEAVING

Suddenly Hu sat up in his bed. Something had awakened him. Although it was still early morning, he could see a crack of gray light under the window shutters. Then he heard it, a deep booming from the direction of Padeng, the firing of heavy guns.

Kaifah awoke then, frightened. "What is it, Hu?"

"There must be fighting up behind the mountain. It sounds near." He jumped from bed, pulling on his clothes. Running through the front room, he remembered it was December 24. Oh, yes, the day before Christmas. He was to have gone to Pak Ngao that evening for a Christmas service. Looking out the porch door he could see the clouds brightening toward the sunrise and behind Padeng, but around the rock itself he spotted nothing. The noise continued, seeming to come from behind the mountain.

By then his father and stepmother stood at the door with him, and his brother Yee had walked into the yard. "Do you see soldiers anywhere?" Yee asked, peering about in the dim light.

Hu looked up and down the village road. "No, I see nothing. It may be the battle that has been threatening for so many days."

"Perhaps you are right," the father observed, "and the insurgents already control Houei Sai."

Pink clouds gathered in the sky, and in Nam Yawn the villagers left their houses to crowd into Hu's yard. Everyone talked at once.

"Has the war come again, you think?"

"Should we prepare to flee today?" a woman called.

"Will there be any shooting here?" another cried.

"Oh, where shall we hide?"

Standing on the porch of his house, Hu looked down at the circle of anxious faces. "This is not the time to flee. We cannot be sure where the fighting is. For now we seem to be safer here. Go back home and stay close by all day."

"That's right," Yee added. "And that means you children, too, must not stray far from your houses."

"Go home," Hu repeated. "Pray that God will keep us safe and help us to know what to do."

The first rays of sunlight touched the hills as the people scattered, some to their homes, others stopping to discuss the situation in low voices. At each distant boom Hu cringed inside. Here and there a child whimpered, and the village dogs slunk around as if someone had kicked them. Hu turned back into his house. "Well, I will not be going to Pak Ngao today."

"No," Kaifah answered, pinning up her hair while she talked. "I fear it will be a sad Christmas. And all the sticky rice and the rice cakes ready too." She sighed deeply.

"It is well that Ahjon Pangan and the American visitors stayed no longer," the mother commented.

"I was only now thinking the same," Kaifah said. "They would be in great danger if they were here now."

"Yes," Hu added from his seat on the doorstep. "God was directing in all. When I met Ahjon Pangan and Mem and her husband last week in Chiang Khong, they asked me first of all if I thought it safe for them to come here. You see, Wanlope had already told them the rumor that Houei Sai might fall at any time. I had been praying about the whole problem and somehow felt it would be possible. 'But only for three days,' I told them. God was leading in that. They arrived the fifth day of last week and departed on the seventh."

"Yes," Kaifah said, "I remember I felt sorry that they left so soon after the baptism on Sabbath, not even stopping to eat. I wanted them to have one more meal with us. But they had to hurry to the dedication of the chapel in Toong Sai, and that's across the river."

"That is right. They had to be there at three o'clock. Americans walk slower than we do. Even the children carrying the luggage got ahead of them. I went on ahead on my new bicycle to tell the boatman to wait, or he might have left without them."

"Well, I'm glad they heard your stories, Hu, and saw our village," the mother said, "because now Mem can write a book about us, and all the people in America will know about Nam Yawn."

"Perhaps they will be the last Americans ever to come here," Hu observed. His voice trailed off, and he turned his head toward Padeng and the thunder of guns.

"Don't be sad, Hu," Kaifah said, kneeling beside him, her arm around his shoulder. "God has promised that His good spirits will keep His children. For many years He has protected us."

"You are right. You speak like one of the good spirits yourself."

Kaifah smiled, then looked at the sky. "Oh, the sun is getting high, and Mother has already started the rice." With a quick kiss on his cheek, she left.

Intermittently all day the roar of the big guns continued, laying a pall of fear over the valley. Evening came and the artillery fell silent at last. The villagers finished their evening meal, and after hushed conversation around the supper fires, settled down for the night.

On the twenty-fifth of December Hu woke again to the noise of gunfire. That morning continued much like the one before, with the village subdued and the children quiet, staying close to their homes. Then by early afternoon the guns ceased.

Hu left his house and walked down the road toward the falling sun. When he had reached the edge of his village, he stopped, glancing about for any signs of activity. Then he saw him—a man in the uniform of a government soldier staggering out from behind a tree. After watching him for a while to make sure he was alone, Hu went over to meet him. As he got closer he could see that one arm hung limp, and blood had soaked through the sleeve of his jacket at the shoulder. The man sank down as if exhausted and sat leaning against a tree, his face ashen. Hurrying over to him, Hu asked, "Are you badly hurt?"

The soldier looked up in surprise. "I was shot in the arm this morning. I have been walking since the early hours. The fighting went bad for us even then. I expect the enemy to have control of that hill by now."

"What hill?"

"Just the other side of Padeng. The one where we had the big guns." The man jerked his head to indicate the direction. "We've been fighting there for two days, but I don't hear the guns now. Probably it's all over. Many men have died defending that hill, and all for nothing." He lifted his good arm to wipe the sweat from his face and sighed deeply. "How much farther is it to the government clinic on the edge of outer Nam Yawn?"

"More than an hour of steady walking. Can you stand up? Here, I'll help you." Lifting him by his good arm, Hu raised the man to his feet. He kept his arm around him, saying, "Lean on me. Then you won't faint."

They moved slowly, and by late afternoon they had reached the small dispensary. Two medics were bandaging a man who had a wounded foot. Several other men with bloodstained clothes and improvised slings and bandages waited their turn. No one said much of anything. Most seemed overcome with pain and exhaustion, and a dull air of defeat hung over them.

Just as Hu started to leave, three men came up carrying an improvised stretcher. On it lay a man in torn, blood-soaked clothes. Hu thought perhaps one of his arms was gone, but he couldn't be sure. The eyes were closed, and the face had such a bloodless pallor that Hu wondered if he still lived. The carriers set their burden down on the floor of the clinic and the medics quickly bent over it. "He is dead," Hu heard them say.

The three who had brought the stretcher emerged from the small building, their faces drawn, their eyes downcast. One of them had a deep, red gash across his cheek, which he seemed to be unaware of. "I told you he was finished," one said.

"Well, he was my friend. I had to be sure."

"Where is the fighting?" Hu asked.

The soldier with the gash on his cheek pointed down the road. "At the Pak Ngao bridge," he said. "There has been fighting all the way to Houei Sai. It started yesterday. We lost some good men at that bridge. I don't know how many." His voice sounded so dull and indifferent that Hu wondered at it.

"Has the fighting stopped at the bridge?"

"Yes, it's over, all right. We never had a chance. They sent our best men to hold the hill beyond Padeng." The soldier turned away, his companions following closely behind.

Hu reached his house by nightfall and reported what he had heard. They heard no more gunfire, and during the night nothing unusual disturbed the stillness. The next morning dawned clear and peaceful. Except for the memory of the gunfire and the wounded men he had seen, it would have been easy to imagine that everything was normal.

In the afternoon Hu set out to investigate once more. In the outer village the clinic was deserted, and Hu saw no villagers whom he could recognize. Soldiers roamed everywhere, all of them wearing the uniform of the invading forces. He noticed one at the crossroads not far from the clinic. The insurgent stood stiffly erect, holding his rifle—his uniform neat, his boots shining.

Hu walked over to him. "Is the fighting over?"

"Yes." The soldier spoke without glancing at him.

"Well, what is happening now?"

"Nothing. Everything is under control." He turned to look at him then. "We're taking care of things. You just go home and stop worrying."

The next day was Friday. That evening as the sunset ushered in the Sabbath, the people of Nam Yawn gathered around their fires to repeat God's promises and to sing the hymns they knew. One by one the houses became silent. At around ten o'clock Hu's dogs started to bark. Soon others answered, until all the dogs in the village joined in the din. Hu peered through the crack under his window shutters. He wasn't sure, but he thought he saw a shadow move as something or someone darted under his house. Turning from the window, he noticed his stepmother who had just been peeking through a crack in the opposite wall. Her lips formed the word "soldiers," but she made no sound, only gestured that someone lurked under the house.

Kaifah nodded, her eyes wide with alarm. "I am glad Father and the baby are asleep," she whispered.

Hu put his finger on his lips, and the three sat in tense silence for what seemed a very long time. All the while the dogs continued their frenzied cries. Finally the sound of the barking moved off, and Hu could barely discern dark forms running along the village road. The barking ceased soon after.

The next morning excited villagers came to church reporting that they, too, had seen prowlers. Those whose houses were built off the ground like Hu's told of men crouching and listening underneath, and two people had spotted strangers moving around the church and school.

"I wonder what they want?" one woman said.

"Why, the thing is clear," Hu's father replied. "They are looking for the Americans who visited here."

"That's right," the church elder agreed, "and you can be sure they'll be back. They will not be satisfied until they are positive that the foreigners are gone."

His word proved true. The soldiers came back that night and the next, crouching and listening.

Monday morning Hu was under his house working on his bicycle when several excited children ran to him. "Soldiers," they shouted, pointing down the road. Hu came out into his yard in time to meet a company of six or seven armed with rifles.

The commanding officer stepped forward. "We have come to find out where you are keeping those foreigners you have here. We saw them come in, but no one saw them leave."

"Why, they left this place long ago," Hu answered. "More than a week ago."

"We don't believe you. You are feeding them in the jungle."

"No," Hu persisted, "we are not. They are gone; thus we cannot be feeding them. Those foreigners were not soldiers anyway. They were missionaries."

"Well, whoever they are," the officer said, waving toward the wooded hillside, "you must be hiding them somewhere around here." He turned toward the church and school. "Look at those wooden buildings. Those are not Meo buildings. The foreigners give you money. They built these buildings."

"We ourselves collected our own money," Hu explained, "and we constructed them to educate our children. Those are not foreign buildings."

"We will see," the commander snapped. He sounded unconvinced. "You don't need to think you can deceive us with any tricks. We are watching you." With that he strode out of the yard and down the road, his men following.

For three weeks the soldiers returned day after day with the same question, and nightly they spied and listened. Their vigils kept a strain on the village, but the people had nothing to hide. As Yee said, "They will watch a long time before they see any Americans around here."

Then one day when the usual group of soldiers arrived, everyone noticed a difference in their attitude. The insurgents were almost jovial, patting the children's heads, even cracking a harmless joke or two. Evidently they seemed convinced at last that Nam Yawn was not harboring spies and were ready to introduce the next stage of their program. The commanding officer asked where he could meet with all the people, and Hu led him to Yee's house, the largest dwelling, and sent word for the people to gather there. Then the military leader began to speak. He had a friendly way about him and spoke confidently. "There is no need for you people to fear anything," he announced. "We are chasing out all foreigners, especially Americans, setting our country free. Everywhere in Laos the struggle goes well. Soon the country will start a new life." Speaking more in the same vein, he then dismissed the people and left with his men.

Squads of soldiers came often after that, always showing friendliness, trying to win the people's confidence. One Sabbath Hu looked up from the pulpit to see several soldiers standing in the doorway. They said nothing, only listened, until the service ended. Afterward they spoke to the people in the churchyard. "You people have no need to worry," the propaganda officer declared. "We represent a government for the people. You can have religious freedom and believe as you like."

The villagers said nothing.

Daytime visits from soldiers continued. One day some of the village men approached Hu quite concerned. "Hu," one man began, "we feel that you are in danger. Those soldiers who were here this morning talked as usual about how we had nothing to fear from them, but later when they did not know we were near, we heard them say, 'We will have to get that preacher one day.' It was not only one of us who heard it, Ahjon. All of us did."

"Well, what do you want me to do?" There was an edge of impatience in Hu's voice.

"Why don't you stay in the jungle for a while? We think it would be safer."

Finally Hu let them persuade him. Taking a blanket, a book, his gun, and ax, he started for the jungle at the edge of the village. He had walked only a short way when he heard a noise behind him and turned to see Keu, his nephew, running to catch up with him, also with an ax and blanket. "I want to come," he told him. "Two are better than one sleeping in the trees."

"If one can guess anything from the big smile on your face," Hu teased, "I think you are only looking for adventure." But Hu was glad for his company. They walked on, soon reaching a place where the trees were thick and the shadows deep. In a short time they had built a platform in a tall spreading tree by tying lengths of bamboo together with vines. From their leafy hideout they could look down among the trees, sleep peacefully, or simply sit and think, all in comparative safety.

The night went by uneventfully, and the next morning Keu went back to the village to get food and to reconnoiter. In the afternoon he returned, saying that no soldiers had come yet that day, but that the people still thought Hu should stay hidden.

The two sat on their platform, munching the rice and chicken Keu had brought. "I like this life," the boy grinned. "This tree, with a roof of leaves and all the birds calling and chattering, makes a good home."

"Yes, it is good enough," Hu said dourly. "But I am wasting precious time here. All morning I have been thinking of our people in Pak Ngao. Ahjon Pangan just baptized four of them, and I have not visited them since. Why, I know nothing of what has happened to them with all this fighting."

"But you can't help anybody if you get yourself shot."

"Then there's Phua in Nam Phet," Hu went on, ignoring Keu's remark. "He begged to know more of Vatiu Yesu several weeks ago, and I have not returned as I promised."

"No doubt he has heard of the fighting," Keu reasoned. "I'm sure he will understand why you haven't come."

"No doubt, no doubt," Hu mimicked. "I tell you I cannot stand this hiding and waiting. It wears out my spirit. I will stay here tonight, but tomorrow if nothing has happened, I will go into the outer village myself and investigate."

Keu looked at him in alarm, shrugged helplessly, and said nothing.

The night passed quietly, and the next day both men climbed down from the platform with their gear and walked back to Nam Yawn. They found the village quite normal, with no visitors; so after a hot meal, Hu set out for the army headquarters in the outer village. A few inquiries brought him to the house he sought, and he soon stood before the commanding officer, a man who looked up with a bored expression.

"My name is Hu Sae Yang, and I have come from Nam Yawn village. I have heard rumors that you intended to capture me, and I have come to ask you if they are true."

The official, who had been sitting listlessly, sat up with a start and looked at the bold young man with interest. "Oh, you're the preacher," he said. "I remember you."

Hu nodded, trying to decide whether the glint in the man's eye held any trace of humor. He decided it did not.

"Why would we want to capture you?" The man's voice carried the trace of a sneer.

"I'm sure I don't know, but I wanted to know what plans you might have."

"My men have already told you that you don't need to worry. We aren't going to take you."

"Well, in that case, I would like to go to Pak Ngao. Some of my people are there, and I need to see them."

"If you want to travel," the officer replied, "you will have to get a travel card and a special permit." The man directed him to another house, and Hu began the process of obtaining travel papers. He had not secured the last one when the office closed for the day; so he had to cycle the nine kilometers home and return the next morning. It was almost noon of the next day before he had everything he needed and could proceed to Pak Ngao.

He had his bicycle on the trip, for the road was quite level as it followed the river. Despite the tedious delays, he felt good to be able to do God's work again. As he pedaled along he thought of the simple church he and a few of the men had just built in Pak Ngao. A typical Meo building with woven bamboo walls, thatched roof, and a floor of neatly packed earth, it would be quite adequate. He had planned to start public evangelistic meetings in the little hall early in the new year, but now he wondered if he would be able to. A few days of fighting had made a great change in his life and in the lives of his people.

Passing the outer houses of the village, he soon came to the public water spout in the central common. Suddenly an excited voice called his name, and he looked up to see one of the two boys who had recently been baptized. "Oh, Ahjon, I am glad you are safe. Is everything well with you there in Nam Yawn?"

"Yes, so far."

When Hu had inquired after everyone and knew everything was all right in Pak Ngao, they walked on together, Hu pushing his bicycle. "Our little church," he asked, "is it still undamaged?" He strained his eyes to see it and quickened his pace as it came into view. The small structure still stood as neat and solid as he had left it. Leaning his bicycle against the front wall, he started to enter the building when he heard footsteps behind him and turned to face two soldiers.

"Do you know about this house?" they asked.

Hu nodded.

"What is this building for and whom does it belong to?"

DEMON OF PADENG

"I and my people built it for a place where we could worship God."

"You are a priest?"

"I am a Christian pastor, and I am not interested in politics. I work only to help my people know and worship God."

"You need not fear us," the soldiers said. "You can worship what you please." Without further discussion they departed.

"We shall see," Hu said, glancing up at the hill behind the church. The bleak outline of an antiaircraft gun met his gaze, giving him the uneasy feeling that his plans for holding meetings in the little church would never materialize.

He stayed the night in Pak Ngao, holding a service in one of the houses in the evening, and returned home the next morning. A few days later he set about to get permission to go to Nam Phet. It took two days, but finally he left, walking as usual because the trail was too steep and rocky for his bicycle. Phua and his family welcomed him with great joy. "We wondered why you delayed so long until we heard about the fighting," Phua said. "Then I feared for your safety, but Kua always reminded me, 'Yesu will care for Hu. He has yet to teach and baptize us.' "

"Yes," Hu smiled, "God has had His hand over our place. And I see things are as usual here."

"Oh, yes," Phua laughed, "except for the spirits. Yesu has commanded them to leave us alone, and they come no more. Many people in the village watch events with much interest."

"I am happy now," Kua stated as she brought out a stool for Hu, and everyone sat down. "It is a happy thing to belong to God. He goes with me everywhere."

Hu watched the joy on her face, and tears came to his eyes as he remembered her former despair.

After supper Hu taught the whole family more about the God they had begun to know, of His promises for every trouble, of His ever-present care.

Kua said, "I know a little about this already. I fear the spirit tree no longer. At night I walk in peace. The noise of the jungle is nothing."

"It is the same with me," the young son spoke up eagerly, his eyes shining. "Last week I heard the cry of the klong-lu-hao, and at first I was afraid, but then I remembered. So I asked Vatiu Yesu to keep me safe, and I wasn't frightened anymore. And I thought of the time when we prayed, and the spirit on the roof ran away, and I laughed and laughed."

They all laughed together, happy in their new security. "I will teach you a new song," Hu said. "You can sing it as you go out to work in your fields."

> "God created the world.
> I turn my ears to listen.
> I hear the insects and birds sing together.
> And I think in my heart
> All these creatures show me
> That God created the world."

It was the first of several visits Hu made to Nam Phet despite the tedious travel requirements and the opposition he met from officials who couldn't understand his need to travel so often.

In February Kaifah got permission to go to Chiang Khong to visit her parents, who came there to meet her. Later Hu also went there. They were away from home two weeks, during which Hu received formal ordination to the ministry. Then they returned to Houei Sai and proceeded home. When they checked in at outer Nam Yawn, the sentry met them with suspicion.

"Why have you been gone so long?"

"We were visiting my wife's parents."

"I don't believe you. You are a spy and have been communicating with the CIA."

"I am not a spy. I am a Christian pastor."

"And your wife, why should she have to go with you and be gone so long? I went to your village last week and found her gone. Our government doesn't want you people leaving the country."

"We are not fleeing, but returning. If we had meant to escape, we would not have come back."

DEMON OF PADENG

"If you are not a spy, why do you travel so much?"

The officer continued his cycle of questioning, often repeating himself to see if Hu would stick to his story. Despite the harassment, Hu continued visiting his people, particularly the family in Nam Phet. Always the authorities interrogated him on his return. Once when he came to ask permission, the usual officer was not there. When the soldier in charge told him bluntly that he couldn't go anywhere, he could do nothing but go back home. When he returned the next day, the familiar officer was there, and, as usual, demanded, "Why do you have to travel around so much and stay so long?"

"I have told you," Hu answered politely. "I am a Christian pastor, and I must visit my people."

"Where is your wife?"

"She is at home."

"I don't believe you. We shall investigate." The officer then sent two soldiers to walk back with Hu to his village to make sure Kaifah was there.

During that time a letter came from the mission inviting Hu to continue his training at the tribal center at Chiengmai. It was something he had wanted to do for a long time, but as he thought about the people in Nam Yawn and Pak Ngao and of the great interest among the inhabitants of Nam Phet, he felt he could not consider leaving until he was sure somebody would carry on his work. He wrote the mission explaining his feelings. They replied that Pau Sae Chang, a young Meo just finishing the ministerial course in Bangkok, would live in Nam Yawn and take Hu's place.

Hu asked God for special guidance. "God in the sky, please help me to know if I am to go. I will stay if You want me to. If the authorities will let Pau come, and the work will not suffer, I will know it is right for me to go to school."

Then with his characteristic frankness, Hu went to the officials who knew him in outer Nam Yawn and told them of Pau's coming. "Are you people going to continue to let us do our work?" he asked. "Do you plan to shut things down later on? I see that you have made all the foreigners leave Houei Sai and other places; so I was wondering."

The officer, now accustomed to Hu's bluntness, said, "Your friend has nothing to fear. We do not stop a man from returning to his own country. If you work here to help your people, we will not bother you. It is only foreigners who are being expelled."

Shortly afterward the authorities relaxed restrictions. Several times Hu managed to enter and leave his village freely, and one day he heard that some Filipino doctors whom the new government had sent away from the Houei Sai hospital had been permitted to return. It seemed that according to the sign he had prayed for, he was being directed to go to school.

Near the beginning of April Pau Sae Chang arrived, and Hu began taking him to meet the various groups of believers. Also a letter from Rangsit in Chiengmai told Hu that classes would begin the first of May, and that he should not be late. It meant that he would have to make the last visit to Nam Phet immediately if he was to leave for school on time.

After securing the required papers, the two pastors started on the long hike. The way seemed shorter than usual as Hu recounted to Pau the story of Phua's deliverance and the interest of the village people in the Creator-God.

The welcome they received could almost have been called tumultuous. Phua's children sped through the village with the news that *two* pastors who had power over the spirits had arrived, and a crowd of curious children and adults soon gathered at Phua's house. They stayed for the evening Bible study and sat attentively around the fire listening to every word and joining with the singing.

Three different men, one an assistant to a spirit doctor, asked the pastors to come and burn the spirits for them in their homes. "We want to be free like Phua," they said. "Why, he has not been sick even once during the past seven months, and the spirits leave him alone. Now we want to belong to your God too." Hu and Pau spent the next day destroying the spirit fetishes at the three houses and, with prayer and song, committing the members of each family to the care of God.

One evening Hu told the people the story of Yesu's baptism in the Jordan and explained its meaning. "Phua and Kua," said Hu, "it is time for you to be baptized now. Baptism is the entrance into God's kingdom. Tomorrow, Phua, you can help me, for we must find a pool of water deep enough for a baptism."

The next day Phua led the pastors along a trail through the jungle for about a kilometer. Along the way Phua turned to Hu and said, "Ahjon, sometimes I am very sad when I think what could have been. If I had only listened to my sister. If I had cast out the spirits when she first told me of true Christianity, Inchow would yet be alive and also my little son."

"Do not talk that way, Phua. Remember what I told you? When Vatiu Yesu comes again He will raise the dead. He will judge them fairly, for He is good. Leave them to Him. Be happy with the good family you have and thank God every day for your deliverance."

"Oh, I do, I do, every day, Ahjon. Listen! Do you hear the roar of water? We are coming to the river."

Suddenly they broke through the trees. Straight ahead a white waterfall dropped over a cliff into a glassy pool that reflected the green of the jungle and the glittering sunlight. "A perfect place," Hu commented.

The next morning was Sabbath and Hu, Pau, and Phua's family led the way to the jungle pool for the baptism, while most of the village followed. The pastors and the candidates stood on a grassy spot by the pool, and the watching people perched on large rocks and boulders around the water's edge, with some of the children even sitting in the trees.

Hu talked to them of the home of the Father in the sky as told about in His Book. He told of the new heaven and earth the Father will make, and how that place will have no more death, sorrow, crying, or ever any pain. And he described the jeweled city and the river of life, crystal clear, coming out of God's throne.

"This river that we see here today is beautiful," Hu said, "but God's river is better because it shines with His glory. There is also a tree of life there, and those who eat of the fruit of it never die again." Many more things he told them about the home of the good Father and of what He has prepared for those that love Him.

"And now," Hu concluded, "I will tell you the promise of Yesu just before He went back to His Father. These were His words. 'Do not let your hearts be sad. . . . In my Father's place there are many houses. I am going there to get a place ready for you, and then I will come back and take you to my own home.' "

After that they sang a song, with Pau leading.

> "I have sinned and fled far from my Father.
> Now I am returning,
> Coming home, coming back home.
> God is not far away.
> Father, teach me to know Your joy.
> Today, I am coming back home."

That evening Phua and his family sat around the fire with Hu and Pau and the three families that had just burned the spirits. They knew it would be their last night together for a long time, and the moments were precious. Hu told them of his plans to go to school. "But I will be back," he told them, "and while I am gone Ahjon Pau will visit you and teach you just as I have done."

The faces around the fire were solemn a moment. Then Phua's little girl spoke up. "But God is not leaving," she said.

Everyone smiled, for nothing could long disturb the peace that surrounded Phua and his family.

Hu gazed into the fire with a faraway look. "I recall the first night I entered this house," he said. "What despair, what darkness!"

Phua laughed. "How well I remember! The words of God say that His children are born again. It is well spoken. I am truly a new man now. Even my leg is like new." And he slapped the once-crippled limb.

Kua rose to put another stick on the fire, then returned to her low stool. The April evening was not cold, but they needed the fire for light. "What Phua says is true for all of us," she said. "It is a good thing to be without fear and to know that nothing can separate us from the Strong One who also is good."

And Hu, looking at the radiant faces in the circle of the firelight, knew that her words spoke also for the others as well.

DEMON OF PADENG

EPILOGUE

Hu and Kaifah and their little boy departed Nam Yawn fully intending to return once Hu finished his course of study, but the political climate of Laos changed drastically soon after they left. The authorities closed the border and greatly limited freedom to come and go. Hu's replacement, Pau Sae Chang, after much harassment and increasing difficulty in doing his work, finally left five months after he arrived, feeling that his life was in danger.

Hu was especially disappointed that Pau never had a chance to return to Nam Phet. Once, about four months after he had left Nam Yawn, Hu was in Chiang Khong, when he encountered a woman relative of Phua from Nam Phet. She reported that the spirits had never returned to torment either Phua or the three families for whom Hu had burned the spirits on his last visit. The woman said that if he could return to Nam Phet, many people would want to study about the Creator-God and be baptized. For Hu it represented news both sad and joyful.

In January of the next year Hu's father died in the village of Toong Sai (near Chiang Khong), where he and his wife had taken refuge. Hu had seen him alive for the last time on a short visit at the New Year. At the funeral Hu met his brother Yee, whom the authorities had permitted to come from Nam Yawn, where he is now the chief. He reported that though some families had left, about one hundred people remained in the village. They were still holding fast their faith, and though they had to listen to government propaganda first, they were permitted to worship each Sabbath.

Hu prays that he may one day return to them.

AUTHOR'S NOTE

Hu recounted most of the various miracles to me, including the spirit healings. Jon Dybdahl, a missionary who knew Hu in Chiengmai, told me of the healing in Chapter 2 and of the log-carrying incident in Chapters 3 and 4. I questioned Hu further to learn exact details. Palmer Wick and Jon Dybdahl described the story of the theft and Hu's discouragement in Chapter 5. All of the miracles in Chapter 7 Hu related to me, and I questioned him particularly about the seventeen families protected from the epidemic in Pak Ngao. I asked if by chance they had access to more or better medicine than the other people. He answered unhesitatingly that, if anything, they had less. The American Aid people in the area who were giving out medicine and supplies in the refugee villages were more inclined to help spirit worshipers than Christians. They reasoned that people adhering to a mission organization would more likely receive other help.

According to Hu, when I saw him last (December, 1975), the little blind girl at the close of Chapter 7 is still in Nam Yawn. Her name is Njai, and no doubt she still walks the paths of Nam Yawn singing of Yesu.

The lack of detail toward the end of Chapter 9 (Hu's ordination, etc.) results from my fear of implicating people who must still work in or near occupied territory. I felt it wiser not to relate Hu's experiences or movements once his country's government changed hands.

GLOSSARY OF MEO WORDS

Ahjon—Pastor
Ai—Brother, as in sense of a church member (Brother Hu); but more especially, Mr.
Baht—Basic monetary unit of Thailand, worth twenty baht to one U.S. dollar at the time mentioned in the story
Da—Spirit
Da-nyu-va—The chief spirit-god
Donyong—A tree consisting of very hard wood
Jai—Spirit appeasement to get rid of sickness
Ketchua—Carrying basket or container
Khene—A bamboo wind instrument played at funerals
Kip—Lao currency, worth two hundred kip to one U.S. dollar at the time mentioned in the story
Klong-lu-hao and **Long-jua**—Birds of evil omen, according to Meo superstition
Padeng—"Red cliff"
Pookheng—Leader or headman
Tu-ua-neng—Witch doctor
Zia da—A ceremony to burn spirit fetishes